The Professional Ghost Investigator

By Jessie Desmond

THE PROFESSIONAL GHOST INVESTIGATOR

Copyright ©2013 by Jessie Desmond

Artwork & Illustrations ©2013 by Jessie Desmond

The Professional Ghost Investigator is a how-to book covering investigation of the paranormal.

Published by:

Alaska Dreams Publishing

www.alaskadp.com

First Printing November, 2013

ISBN numbers:

ISBN-13: 978-0-9855588-8-8

ISBN-10:0985558881

eBook Available

This book has been written
for anyone interested in
ghost investigation.
It is a book of standards.

Table of Contents

Dedication

I'd like to dedicate this
book to Ty Keltner, my partner
in crime when it comes to
paranormal research.

Acknowledgments

I'd like to take a minute to thank some people who helped me with my quest since birth to figure out the truths behind paranormal occurrences.

First off, I'd like to thank my parents for letting me have a wandering mind, but encouraging me to find solid answers for my questions. I'd also like to thank everyone who was in my 4th grade Ghost Hunters club. Stories were shared and interest only grew. Thank you Ty Keltner, who became my investigation and research partner back in 2001. Thank you former members of PEAK for your dedication to the paranormal. Finally, thank you James Zarones for our early childhood bet of who will have the first book published. I win!

Introduction

Over the course of the last 14 years I have gone from being an amateur paranormal investigator to a professional. My beginnings were in ghost investigation, but have since spread to encompass anything in the realm of the unknown, the occult, and the paranormal. I have spent time looking for cryptids. I am a field investigator for MUFON (the Mutual UFO Network). I have gone to great lengths to research old and ancient methods of dealing with the paranormal and demonology. Much to my dismay, I have found that there are many amateurs out there who give this field of fringe science a bad name.

This book is designed to give other investigators in the field of Paranormal Studies a particular set of standards and instructions simply on Ghost Investigation. The reader will walk away with a full understanding of the standards, knowledge of terms and equipment, a bibliography that doubles as a suggested reading list, the ability to get rid of ghosts in a basic sense, and how to properly conclude your cases. Most other books on this subject are not as in-depth and often leave readers with many unanswered questions about basic techniques, goals, and standards. You will find that each chapter contains anecdotes, activities, guides, and brief quizzes.

If you find yourself completely intrigued or wanting more, then I encourage you to start checking into older texts. You may have to learn a little bit of Latin or French along the way. Don't let that stop you. Learn all you can. Explore. Assist others as you become capable.

Talking about my investigations has always been a strange grey area. Sure, I have seen ghosts and shadow people, among other things, but discussing these things with most people has a tendency to make a person appear a little crazy or susceptible to ideas of fancy. Through this book I have attempted to create a more stable perception on ghost investigation by focusing on remaining objective. Try to figure out if it's a noisy pipe before you assume it's a ghost, know what I mean?

One thing that people usually want to know about me is: how did I ever get started in this field. Three simple answers: *Ghostbusters*, Alvin Schwartz' *Scary Stories to Tell in The Dark* trilogy, and *Beetlejuice*. I was always into reading about spooky occurrences, horror, mystery, and history. As a kid I read every book available from the library on ghosts. I had a group of friends who were also into ghosts and other areas of the paranormal, so we traded oral stories and books and art.

Over the years I wanted to know more about why ghosts were around and how they could be put to rest. I also started looking into urban legends and tales of teenage horror from those daring enough to use the Ouija board. This led into researching the rise of witchcraft, black arts, and Satanism in the 1960s up to the present date. I knew that if I was going to continue looking into this particular field I had to start looking into how to protect myself from these entities. Some of them are fairly harmless, but some of them can be real bastards.

I am aware that this introduction reads somewhat like a warning; it is one. If you're interested in ghost investigation at all, you need to take heed of the warnings. This isn't a glamorous field as you might expect from *Ghostbusters* or the reality television shows. In fact, I guarantee you some very long and boring nights. Just be prepared for the worst, remain professional, and always follow through with a case. There's a good chance that you will never be paid for your services, but they will be needed.

Before I cut this introduction short, I want to quickly emphasize community and collecting data. The world of ghost investigation is a little jumbled. If there was a greater sense of community I fully believe that there would be more breakthroughs in understanding ghosts and hauntings. This is why, in this book, I will propose a new way to create a sense of community. Also, when you don't have a case, start collecting data about old cases in your area. Perhaps there's a bit of research that can be done about a local ghost that everyone knows about. Always look for data to collect.

Onwards and Upwards!
Jessie Desmond

Chapter 1 –Investigating Basics

Investigating ghostly phenomenon is not something that everyone should participate in. The work usually does not pay, the hours are long, days and months can pass between cases, and the professional ghost investigator has to be on the constant look out for amateurs and skeptics. This chapter is designed to give you an overview of ghost investigation and what it means to be a professional ghost investigator including: practicing the trade, objectivity, appearance, finding a team, finding a meeting place, and GI etiquette. These are all very basic norms every investigator needs to follow and respect.

Ghost investigation is the act of researching, collecting evidence, understanding the evidence, and attempting to find a conclusion with spiritual, afterlife, and, often, psychic activity. Ghosts and psychics often go hand in hand since there is an element of spiritual communication that can take place during investigations.[1] Most ghost investigation is based on research, the scientific process, and attempting to provide closure for the client.

Ghost investigators typically take on cases dealing with ghosts and hauntings, house blessings/spiritual blessings, local history of specific people and places, spirit photography, psychic testing, and spiritual communication. You'll find that many professional ghost investigators are psychologists, photographers, historians, and scientists. These professions

---

[1] Chapter 4 - Psychics

lead themselves to serious research into the mysterious world of spiritualism, ghost investigation, and psychic phenomenon.

Professional vs. Amateur

Simply put, amateur investigators treat ghost investigation as nothing more than a hobby. Their methods are sloppy, their fellow investigators have little or no knowledge of their current case, and they often experience group hysteria which is interpreted as a ghostly encounter. Almost all professionals started out as amateur investigators running around a local cemetery with a camera and a voice recorder.

Professional investigators use specific procedures in order to ensure uniformity to their investigations, they do a ton of research before and after an investigation, and they are constantly paying attention to ongoing theories about spiritual and psychic activity. Professional investigators are not afraid to publish their findings, as long as they have client permission, and they provide their clients with a copy of their findings. A good investigator will put their beliefs aside and work on a case as unbiased as possible. This means that any Christian, Jewish, Muslim, Hindu, pagan, or magical practices need to be set aside. As an investigator a person must remain neutral in order to be taken seriously.

Amateurs might form a group or a club where they gather once or twice a month for official meetings where they attempt to discuss ghosts. This usually turns into gossip and/or a chat session between friends. Professionals will have meetings amongst their members and will run it in a professional manner with minutes and workshops.

It is perfectly okay to have an amateur investigation group who wants to keep things on a hobby-level. If you only have the time for an amateur-level group you won't have people take you seriously, you won't be bogged down with research, and you can keep ghost investigation to the weekends. Professionals, if they keep to their standards and follow this book, will be able to publish their findings, satisfy clients, and will essentially have a finished product at the end of each investigation. Throughout this book, you will find the differences between the professional and amateur. By the end of this book, you should be able to become more professional, amateurs will be able to have a better understanding of the field, and everyone will have a set of standards to follow for the field.

Practice & Objectivity

Practice of the trade is a key element for any professional. For a ghost investigator, practicing might include going to your favorite cemetery using a single piece of equipment, reading trade magazines for equipment or paranormal practices, talking and learning from local professionals about pieces of equipment (like photographers or audio technicians), and keeping in shape so you can perform your investigations with ease. Many amateurs will simply purchase a piece of equipment, will not practice with it or even read the instructions, typically because they have "seen it on tv" or "in a movie". By practicing with your own equipment, you will start to learn about the flaws of your equipment, settings to use, what you are good at using and what you are bad at, whether or not you need any additional pieces for your equipment (like lenses or microphones), and other such things.

Objectivity is the key to a successful investigation and career as a ghost investigator.

Being objective will allow you to approach every case with a professional manner. The goal behind ghost investigation is to attempt to prove the existence of ghostly phenomenon, the presence of an afterlife, the discovery of how to go about detecting and recording spiritual activity in a repeatable manner, and research on psychic activity.

> **Objective** *adj.* **1.** Existing as an object or fact, independent of the mind; real. **2.** Determined by the realities of the thing dealt with rather than the thoughts of the writer or speaker. **3.** Without bias or prejudice.[2]

Objective investigators are often accused of being skeptical. Shrug it off. Your objectivity keeps you more alert on investigations, more observant, and more apt to flush out the hoaxes and rumors.

During your note taking, you will find that your objectivity will come in handy. You will produce better reports and will gain more respect among the intellectual community. It will be one of the strongest determining factors of your level of professionalism. Be sure to stress *objectivity* to your fellow investigators and new recruits.

Subjective thinking is the complete opposite of **objective** thinking. It's based on personal beliefs, perspectives, feelings, and desires. Most of the academic world, who you are trying to gain the respect of, does not use subjective thinking because it is does not lead to strong methods of theory, purpose, experimentation, and research. Keep subjective thinking out

> **Subjective** *adj.* Of or resulting from the feelings of the person thinking; not objective; personal.[3]

---

[2] "Objective." *Webster's New World Dictionary and Thesaurus*. Michael Agnes, Editor in Chief. Hungry Minds, inc: New York, 2002. 2nd edition.

[3] "Subjective." *Webster's New World Dictionary and Thesaurus*. Michael Agnes, Editor in Chief. Hungry Minds, inc: New York, 2002. 2nd edition.

of your work.

One of the best ways to get your team thinking objectively is to run through a few objectivity exercises as part of your meetings. The rules are to remain objective which means no religion, no racism, no sexism, no other biases allowed; as well as being able to back up your statements, theories, and conclusions with evidence.

In Appendix I I have included a series of questions designed to help your team think objectively. There are not right or wrong answers. If you feel that you should invest in a book on objectivity, I recommend:

Gaukroger, Stephen. *Objectivity: A Very Short Introduction.* Oxford University Press: Oxford, 2012.

Anecdote

When I was running PEAK (Paranormal Explorers of Alaska) with my friend Ty Keltner, we would take people to one of two "in town" cemeteries in order to run them through some equipment basics. We often made trips to the cemeteries during the summer months just to train new people, to learn about new equipment, to practice using current equipment, and to try out new techniques. Our practice sessions were never about finding anything, though it was always awesome when we would get an orb or an EVP. Don't let your training sessions turn into a spur-of-the-moment ghost investigation.

Back in the spring of 2001 I had picked up a brand new voice recorder. Spring in Alaska is usually pretty frigid, the snow is slushy, and the sun stays out until around 5pm. I had the bright idea of venturing out to Birch Hill Cemetery despite the fact that I was wearing a long skirt. The cemetery was closed for the winter, so I had to park at the bottom of the hill and hike up the hill through the

---

knee-deep slushy snow. I had on my combat boots, so I grabbed my voice recorder, locked my car, and trudged up the hill.

I spent about 30 minutes or so making my way up to the main road of the cemetery while talking into my recorder. I'm not sure how many times I asked "Is there anyone with me right now?" and other such questions, but it was quite a bit. I had enough of making way through the slush after my boots started filling with snow. My goal during this cold spring cemetery hike had been to learn what my new recorder could pick up. On my way home I found out, I definitely found out.

Home was not too far away, but the roads were slick and busy so I took my time. I cranked up the volume of the voice recorder and let it play while I made my way home. At one point I asked "Is anyone here with me now?" and, at a very low volume, a female voice clearly said "Hi". After nearly swerving off the road, I made it home and replayed the voice recorder over and over again.

Always be prepared to find something, but always be prepared to find nothing. Equipment testing can prove beneficial, but should not be considered concrete proof since it's just a testing period.

Looking the Part

Your wardrobe choices are another important factor for any professional ghost investigator. When you do your preliminary work and your post-investigation work, including your presentation to your client, you need to look the part. Most investigators go with a "business casual" look. This may be a clean, fairly new pair of jeans, shiny leather shoes, and a blouse or a button-down shirt. It may be a conservative skirt, a sweater, and a pair of heeled-oxfords. You don't need to be in a full-suit or a cocktail dress, but you don't want to show up in worn jeans and a t-shirt either.

When you are doing your actual investigation, you will need to dress for your location. This will be discussed further in Chapter 7, but just be aware that if you are going to be outside at night for 6 hours you should bring a sweater and a jacket. You may even want to wear a pair of thermal tights under what you are wearing for additional heat. Be sure that you have the proper footwear, that even with gloves you can still use your equipment, and that everyone is aware of the type of clothing to bring along.

Aside from clothing, you will also want to physically look as if you can handle the investigation. If you are investigating a large cemetery on a hill, you will need to be able to manage yourself. You don't want to be breathing heavy if you have a video camera or a voice recorder because it might be misinterpreted when you review your findings. An efficient ghost investigator will be in good physical shape in order to prevent misinterpretations of findings, physical problems during investigations (like shortness of breath, stamina issues, moving around various places, etc), and to help ensure a better reception from the client.

Finding Your Team

The process of finding a proper team is a long hard road. You will come across a few different types of people and it's ideal to be able to spot them. If you are starting from scratch or simply with a partner, and have the intention of adding to your numbers, here are a list of things to look for in your fellow investigators:

Interest – It goes without saying that if you have people applying for a position in your ghost investigation team they are going to have an interest in the subject. You want to make sure that their interest won't wane in a month or two.

Research Skills – Your team members must be proficient researchers. It's best to put them to the test on this one. Don't take them at their word. This is a vital part of the entire process of ghost investigation. You absolutely don't want a person who is simply "not interested in research".

Education and Skills – If your team members all have their Bachelor's degrees, or higher levels of education, it will reflect well on your team. If your team members have certain skills, certifications, or training it will also reflect well on your team. If your team is a bunch of high school kids and house-wives your team won't come off as being knowledgeable or highly regarded.

Age – You want to aim for those people who are in college, but who aren't too old to get out and about. Some groups will have an age range of 18-60, though it's also common to see a range from 21-60. As you can see, the low side of the age range is usually set to 18 (legal adult) or 21 (drinking age). Before you even consider potential team members, you will need to make sure they fit into your age range.

Health – You want to find members who aren't hypochondriacs, who can easily hike up a hill or fit into a small spot, and who won't be "out" due to a constant reoccurring sickness or physical injury. Don't just dismiss people who have medical issues though. You might find that your best investigator is the guy recovering from cancer or the girl with multiple sclerosis.

Dedication – Finding members who are truly dedicated is like pulling teeth; it's tough, its often painful, and when you do find them they might have a tough exterior. Your ultimate goal here is to find people who won't treat what they're doing like a secondary activity. You're not forming a dainty club;

you're forming an investigative team. You'll get hang ups with many students and parents on this. They will neglect research for school purposes, children, for other activities, etc. Stay away from the people who always seem to have an excuse not to do something.

When you decide to start looking for people it is best to first ask for a resume. If you do not receive a resume from a person, you can either tell them that you require it or you can just forget that they are interested. Remember, if they are really interested, they will follow the directions. Be sure to have a particular size limit to your group, perhaps 6-15 members total.

On the resumes, you will want them to include any important medical/health information including allergies. You will also want education, skills, and a brief statement on why they are interested and why they think they'd be a good ghost investigator. The resumes you receive will be your first line of weeding out the bad seeds. Are they too young? Are they physically capable of investigating? Do they have any important or useful skills? Do they seem too busy with other activities to dedicate time to ghost investigation?

With those who pass your first round of weeding, you will want them to show you that they indeed have the ability to do some research. Ask them to research an event that is familiar and fairly local, but provide them with vague information. Have them keep a bibliography using MLA or Chicago style, and give them a page limit typically one or two pages.

Example

Research the following topic and keep a bibliography using Chicago style.

The Van Gilder Hotel in Seward, Alaska is reportedly

---

haunted by a lady. A lady was shot and killed in the hotel by her husband in the 1950s.

Bibliography example:

Zemach, Heidi. "Novelist Promotes Book, Hotel, and Its Ghost." *Seward City News*. September 10, 2010. Accessed online 5/7/2012.
http://sewardcitynews.com/2010/09/novelist-promotes-book-hotel-and-its-ghost/

Once you have a piece of research work done by them you will need to analyze it. Read it over and look for: information and history provided, new information found, the type of sources they used, pictures, check their sources, and look for recommendations that are listed. You will want to have a meeting with them so you can discuss their research and have the final part of the interviewing process.

Be sure to ask them about their researching process, what they found to be interesting, and who they would recommend talking to about a case like the one they researched. Ask them about their education, skills, and any other activities they have. Can they pull an all-night job? Can they properly research for cases? Do they have any other obligations? Will they be able to treat ghost investigating as a job rather than as a hobby?

Meeting Place

You are going to need a place to meet. Most groups meet once a week or once every two weeks. You are absolutely going to need a reliable meeting location with internet access, a table, and enough seating for your members.

If you are not able to rent an office, you can always transform a basement into an investigation office. You also can usually reserve a room at your local library, the Department of Parks & Recreation usually have rentable rooms in some of their facilities, and hotel conference rooms. Despite where you meet, you will have to create a place where you keep your files, this could be at your home on your personal computer or at a private investigation office, but you need to make it secure. A private office may become a space for storing everyone's equipment and might lead to your team to accept itself in a more professional manner. A private office also gives your clients a physical place to meet you, you can accept mail there, a phone line can be installed, paranormal-related experiments can take place here, and your members can talk openly without fear of ridicule.

Ghost Investigator Etiquette

There is a short list of etiquette followed by many investigators. These are not firm rules to follow, but they are guidelines for remaining professional and courteous. Points of etiquette will be listed with an explanation following.

Client-Investigator Privacy – Your client needs to be reassured that their claim will be kept private unless they give you permission otherwise. This is done simply by asking your client to sign a privacy form (see Appendix II).

Talk Professionally – During your time with your client, you will have to speak professionally. They don't need to be impressed by science talk or what you have found in the past. They do need to be reassured that you can deal with their problem. Keep all television talk to your personal time, not your client's time. Attempt to remove slang and colloquialisms from your speech when you are talking to your client. Don't "trash talk" any other group or person(s) during this time.

Contact Other Paranormal Groups – It's not essential, but it is a professional courtesy to keep on good terms with other paranormal groups in your state or region. You may start sharing information, you may decide to hold a conference with some other groups, and you might recommend or receive a recommendation to/by another group. Essentially, you need to think of this as any other business industry. Occasionally there are BBQs or industry get-togethers where people from that particular industry are invited in a neutral manner.

Look and Act Professionally – It's important to look and act the part of the paranormal investigator. The general rule is that when in doubt, stick to business casual. The only exception to this rule is when you are on your investigation, where you ought to dress for the location.

Acting professional is also important for ghost investigators. Your clients will not want someone who is goofy or too creepy or too weird or melodramatic to be dealing with their case. They want someone who is objective, knowledgeable, and organized. A part of acting professional is being punctual. It's best to be 5 minutes early than to be 5 minutes late. Aside from your client appreciating punctuality, you will find that the less familiar you are with certain areas, buildings, or routes, the better off you are by being early.

Explain To The Client – Your client will not understand or know what exactly is going on with their case. You need to do your client a favor and explain what you are doing, what your findings are, what is going on, what their options are, etc. in a non-patronizing way. The best example of this is to think of how a doctor talks to a patient. They are given a problem by their patient, they run tests, do some research, and tell the patient what they think is going on and how they think it can be solved. Just remember to stay objective, define terms that the client doesn't understand, and stay on task. Try not to spread fear. If your clients are the parents of children, it is best to only talk to the parents when discussing your case – unless a child is directly involved and you feel that they need to understand what is going on. Don't get angry at the client for not knowing terms common to you.

Keep Your Beliefs At Home – This is related to remaining objective. Keep your beliefs at home. As a ghost investigator, your religious, social, political, and other beliefs become null and void while on a case. You need to be prepared to do a house blessing according to a variety of religious and cultural methods. You need to understand that your client might be a practicing Catholic, Muslim, Satanist, Baptist, or of no religion at all. They might be democrat, republican, a tree-loving hippie, or a prudent widow. Your beliefs do not matter during your case, except for your own personal state of mind. Ask the client's permission to use rituals and methods that may be problematic.

Chapter 1 Quiz

Define:

Ghost Investigation

Objectivity

Subjectivity

Questions

What are some of the differences between a professional and amateur ghost investigator?

Why is it important to remain objective on a case?

What is the goal of ghost investigation?

How should you dress when meeting a client? Why?

What 6 key points should you look for in potential team members?

What are the 6 key points of ghost investigator etiquette?

Chapter 2 – Equipment of the Investigator

This section highlights the tools of the trade of any ghost investigator. Some of these items you will absolutely need, but some you will not. Many "how to" books often give you a list of items that you should tote around, including this one, but I will answer the why and how as well. I'll start with the standard equipment, the specialized equipment, and research resources.

Standard Equipment

Standard Equipment for a ghost investigation is what you will need for every case. If you're going to investigate a case, these are must-have items or your case will fail. Be sure to invest in a durable equipment case or bag. Some investigators prefer a hard shell case like a brief case or a tackle box, but others use duffle bags or large camera cases. You want to avoid your equipment rolling around, getting lost, and becoming scuffed up.

Paper, Pen, Pencil

It seems rather simple, but these are vital to any investigator. You never know when you need to take notes, draw something, take a statement, jot down the time, or leave someone a note. It also helps during interviews if you don't have to ask for paper and a writing utensil. During an interviewing process, you might want to carry a set of basic colored pencils or markers in case your client wants to draw and color what they have seen.

Colored chalk, pressed charcoal, and china markers/grease pencils can be used for marking areas of sightings, especially if you are measuring or mapping something out. If you ever need to do a rubbing and all you have is a mechanical pencil and an ink pen, you won't be able to get it. By laying a piece of paper upon the object you want to take an impression of and then, with a little pressure, rubbing chalk or charcoal over the paper, you will find yourself with a rubbing that you can take with you. This works well with headstones, crests or symbols on tombs or in houses, and for taking flat impressions of items.

Recommended: Mechanical pencil, black ink pen, set of 8 colored pencils, sketch book, white chalk, blue chalk, pressed charcoal, and a red china marker.

Standard Small Equipment

There are a few random items that need to be mentioned because they are often overlooked. These are common household items that you need to have with you on all cases.

- First Aid Kit
- Wristwatch
- Matches or Lighter
- Pocketknife
- Batteries
- Aspirin/Headache Pills
- Ziploc bags

These items may seem overly common and not important, but these are the common items that are needed on many cases. Definitely invest in a wristwatch, even if it's only for investigations. A cell phone may ring or throw light around. If you want to take your cell phone, only have it with you for emergency purposes only. Some people also take a small candle in case their flashlight dies out and their spare batteries are drained, both of which often happen.

EMF Detector

An **EMF meter** (or **EMF detector**) is a scientific instrument for measuring electromagnetic fields. *EMF* may be an abbreviation for *electromagnetic field* or *electromagnetic fluctuation*. Most meters measure the electromagnetic radiation flux density (DC fields) or the change in an electromagnetic field over time (AC fields). There are many different types of EMF meters, but the two largest categories are single axis and tri-axis. Single axis meters are cheaper than tri-axis meters, but take longer to complete a survey because the meter only measures one dimension of the field. Single axis instruments have to be tilted and turned on all three axes to obtain a full measurement. A tri-axis meter measures all three axes simultaneously, but these models tend to be more expensive.

Electromagnetic fields can be generated by AC or DC currents. An EMF meter can measure AC electromagnetic fields, which are usually emitted from manmade sources such as electrical wiring, while Gauss meters or magnetometers measure DC fields, which occur naturally.

The theory behind the use of the EMF detector is that spiritual energy will raise the level of the local electromagnetic fields, thus being detectable by an EMF detector. With a little searching you will find that there are a few types of EMF meters out there. Some have external sensors, some simply have a digital or analog display, and some use a visual display like the K2 EMF meter. It is best if you can test out a few

31

different types of EMF meters before making a purchase, but most investigators have a variety in their arsenal.

Equipment Test:

When you get your EMF detector, make sure there are batteries in it and turn it on. Your read-out, whether digital or analog, will most likely be 0.0. Go around your house slowly, keeping your EMF detector fairly level if it's analog, and note the readings you get at the following common places:

Refrigerator_____

Bed_____

Kitchen Sink_____

Bath Tub/Shower_____

Inside Wall_____

Outside Wall_____

Closet_____

Circuit Breaker Box_____

Couch_____

Computer OFF_____

Computer ON_____

Microwave_____

Television_____

Stove_____

Dresser_____

Window_____

Most of these places will have the same reading, but make note of where you found different readings. When you use your EMF detector you will need to remember to look for any objects that may cause higher readings to occur. Is there a refrigerator on the other side of the wall? Is that microwave plugged in? What causes the readings that you are getting?

Recommended: An EMF meter.

Flashlight

A **flashlight** is a portable electric spotlight that emits light from a small incandescent light bulb or from one or more light-emitting diodes (LEDs). Flashlights won't set off an EMF detector and are always one of the most useful items to have on an investigation.

When choosing a quality flashlight make sure to check for light equality, quality of light, ease of use, and battery life. Light equality is the even quality of the light produced. Cheap flashlights usually have a focused area of bright light surrounded by a darker area of lesser light. A flashlight with good light equality will provide a solid, or close to solid, area of light. The quality of light should be strong. Cheap flashlights have weak light quality like a 60-watt bulb compared to a 120-watt bulb. Ease of use and the battery life are both fairly self-explanatory. Just be sure that you can use the flashlight with your eyes closed and that your battery life is long lasting.

Recommended: A high quality flashlight.

Voice Recorder

A **voice recorder** is a sound recording device most commonly used to record speech for later playback or to be typed into print. Voice recorders often use

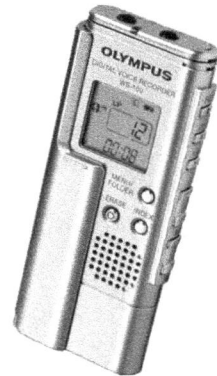

micro-cassettes or are completely digital. They work as audio equipment usually does with record, play, rewind, fast forward, and stop buttons.

Electronic voice phenomena (EVP) are electronically captured sounds that resemble speech, but are not the result of intentional voice recordings. Common sources include static, stray radio transmissions, and background noise. Some people claim these sounds are of paranormal origin, while there are natural explanations such as *apophenia* (finding significance in insignificant phenomena), *auditory pareidolia* (interpreting random sounds as voices in their own language), equipment glitches, or simple hoaxes. Recordings of electronic voice phenomena are often created from background sound by increasing the gain (i.e. sensitivity) of the recording equipment.

Be sure to have an audio program available for editing your audio. Go through the tutorial for the program you choose so you know what you are doing.

Equipment Test:

When you get your voice recorder, load batteries into it and turn it on. Be sure to have the instructional booklet available. You should run through the following tests so you know how your equipment works:

☐ Start a new recording session by stating your name, where you are, the date, and the time.

☐ Speak directly into the voice recorder.

☐ Place the voice recorder 10 feet away from you and talk in a normal tone.

☐ At 10 feet, shout something.

☐ Walk around outside down a busy street.

☐ Walk around outside through a park or nature trail.

☐ Go to a crowded area.

☐ Set the recorder 5 feet away and drop a pencil or pen, a book, a metal pot, and a shoe.

When you play back your recording, make note of how noises sound at the various distances and places. You will have to become familiar with how sounds can start to sound like other things, how voices can carry, and what denotes "normal vocal tones".

Recommended: A handheld voice recorder.

Photography Camera

A **photography camera** is a device that records still images and comes in a few different forms.

Point and shoots come in digital and manual forms. These cameras allow you to simply aim your camera and click a button to take a picture. There is little or no focusing available. Most people own a *point and shoot* camera because they are small, they might be on your phone, or you have one of those disposable 35mm cameras.

SLR (single-lens reflex) *cameras* come in manual and digital forms. They have changeable lenses, manual focusing options, and allow the operator to have the most possible control over their photographs.

Instant cameras are another form of camera, the most popular being a Polaroid Instant Camera. You simply load your film, point the camera, take a picture, the film comes out and in minutes you have a physical picture in your hand.

There is some debate over digital vs. manual cameras. From my experience both can work and both have problems. Your 35mm might capture a great image, but the film developers might ruin your negatives which ruins your photographs. Digital can simply be uploaded to your computer. I have found that while I still use my 35mm, it is easier to use my digital camera. I don't have to change film and it's much easier to go through in the post-investigation process. Whichever camera you decide to use, be sure you know how to use it properly.

Equipment Test:

When you get your camera make sure that you have film loaded or the proper storage card inserted. Make sure that you have a full battery or new batteries. You should run through the following tests so you know how your equipment works:

☐ Take a picture of the same object in every mode available on the camera.

☐ Take a picture of a person inside under good light, under poor light, and in the dark.

☐ Take a picture of an object in dim light with and without your flash.

☐ Go outside during the day and take photos of tree tops, the grass, moving cars, still cars with a moving person, and of a person in the sunlight.

☐ Go outside at night and take a photo of a grassy field, tree tops, a person, a moving vehicle.

When you go back through your pictures, you should notice how objects can look different with different lighting, how dust can affect a picture, how objects or people in motion look compared to still objects or people, and you should be able to start selecting a few favorable camera settings to use. Most people have a few settings they prefer for different types of locations.

Recommended: A camera.

Video Camera

A **video camera** is a camera used for capturing moving images which create a film. Many digital cameras have video options available, but you will want a stationary video camera for investigations. You may even want a few different types for various types of investigations.

The type of video camera that you will want will record either to a tape or, preferably, to a flash card. Flash cards allow your video to be uploaded directly to your computer. You will also want a camera with an audio jack. This will allow you to hook up microphones.

You may also want to consider a motion activated camera. These are usually used by sportsman and can be found at sporting goods stores for roughly $150-$200 on the average. Other cameras that you might want to consider are helmet cameras and surveillance cameras for multi-location investigations.

Be sure that you have some kind of video software that you can use for editing down your video. There are a lot of programs out there that are easy to use. If you purchase one, be sure to run yourself through the included tutorial program so you know what you are doing. Don't forget to buy a tripod

---

Equipment Test:

When you get your video camera, load a fully charged battery and turn it on. Be sure to have the instructional booklet available. You should run through the following tests so you know how your equipment works:

- ☐ Manually set your white balance if the option is available. Use a piece of white computer paper.

- ☐ Press 'record' and walk around the room with your camera in hand.

- ☐ Attach the camera to a tripod, press 'record', and walk around the room while holding the tripod.

- ☐ Set the camera on the tripod and record yourself in front of the camera talking.

- ☐ Hook up a microphone and record yourself talking while the microphone is hooked up.

- ☐ Zoom in as far as you can go, zoom out as far as you can go.

- ☐ Change your settings on your camera. Try out sepia tone, black and white, etc.

When you play back your footage, be sure that you make note of the settings that you prefer to use. Most people forget or don't know how to white balance their cameras. Professionals white balance every time. It makes the white's white and the black's black. I do not recommend relying on auto-white balance.

Recommended: At least one video camera and a tripod.

Thermometer

A **thermometer** is a device that measures temperature or temperature gradient using a variety of different principles. A thermometer has two important elements: the temperature sensor in which some physical change occurs with temperature, plus some means of converting this physical change into a value. Thermometers increasingly use electronic means to provide a digital display or input to a computer.

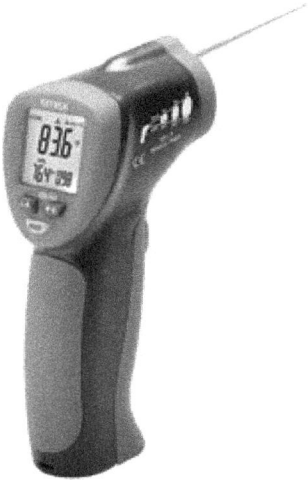

There are three types of thermometers: a standard thermometer, a digital thermometer, and an IR thermometer (shown). Standard thermometers are made of glass or plastic and have red liquid that rises or falls along the C/F degrees. A digital thermometer is a thermometer with a digital readout. It measures the immediate area. The IR (Infrared) thermometer is useful in the field because you basically point it at the area you want to check the temperature of and click on the trigger button. A laser pointer is attached so you can visibly see where you are pointing the thermometer.

Recommended: A digital thermometer and an IR thermometer.

Specialized Equipment

Specialized equipment is not typically used on most cases and can be quite expensive. It's best to be comfortable with the standard equipment before attempting to utilize any specialized equipment on a case. If you are able to work with specialized equipment, be sure to test it out multiple times before using it for a case.

FLIR Camera

Forward Looking Infrared (FLIR) cameras are thermal imaging cameras. They are used as a visual tool for seeing temperature differences in what they are aimed at, detecting gas leaks, and for assistance in seeing in the dark. The theory behind using a FLIR camera is that cold spots, classic indicators of ghosts, may be detectable on such a camera. These cameras are expensive which make them hard to obtain, but they are handheld and are not difficult to operate.

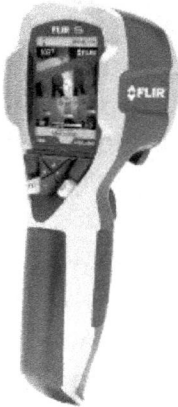

Ovilus, or White Noise Machine

A white noise machine is a very simple machine that produces ambient, or white, noise. White noise machines are not very expensive and are often used to assist with people going to sleep, going into a trance, in music production, and sound masking. White noise has a very broad wave spectrum and is thought by many ghost investigators to assist in obtaining more and clearer EVPs on voice recording equipment.

Motion Sensor Devices

Typically motion sensor devices will emit a noise or have a light pop on when something passes in front of the sensor. Ghosts have been known to set off motion sensors which makes this inexpensive item a great tool on indoor investigations. Setting up a motion sensor in a highly frequented area monitored by a video camera on a tripod can provide some key results.

Research Tools

Part of your equipment is your primary researching tools. Many books on "how to be a ghost hunter" will briefly, if at all, mention this. One thing that separates the professionals from the amateurs is the research. Professional ghost investigators have a whole list of sources they check for nearly every case they work on with a bunch of sources for various types of cases. If you are not into research, then you should NOT be a ghost investigator. Research is a major portion of this line of work. Below is a guide for finding your own primary researching tools. As a rule, these places might seem obvious, but many amateurs don't think of looking in some, if any, of these places.

Public Library - Your local public library will have local information and resources, including local magazines, newspapers, dissertations, historical research, and more. This is always a great place to start any research. Start asking for assistance from the librarians. Part of their job is to assist in finding library material.

Department of Records – This is a government office of public records and sometimes it goes by a few different names like Office of Vital Records or DNR Recorder's Office. You will find public records on land, deeds, and other important non-private filed paperwork.

County or Borough Property Database – This is a database that allows people to pay taxes on their property and also list the current owner(s) of the property. There is usually a property assessment listed as well.

Historical Society – Your local historical society will have a bunch of available information on historical locations. It's usually a positive move to get on the good side of your local historical society. Try to attend a function in order to properly network.

Local Historians – Local historians always have a wealth of information, but they are typically busy people. Unless you are good friends with a local historian, you should approach them after you've done some initial research. They don't always have information on what you want, but sometimes its research gold.

Digital Archives – Digital archives are sometimes run by the state, sometimes by libraries, and sometimes by universities. Most places have them, but the smaller the town, the less likely you are to find one specifically for that area. Most states do have a digital archive of some kind where you will find photographs and video footage from the past.

Private Archives – It takes some digging and networking, but sometimes you can find someone with their own personal archives or private collections.

Chapter 2 Quiz

Questions
1. List at least 5 pieces of standard equipment.
2. List the 3 pieces of specialized equipment.
3. Can you come up with something else that could be used as specialized equipment?
4. List at least 5 research tools.
5. Can you come up with a different research tool for your local area?

Exercise

Test every piece of equipment that you have available to you. If you are working with a partner or in a group, record your readings and compare them to the group's findings. What two or three pieces of equipment do you feel best about using? What do your teammates feel best about using?

Chapter 3 – Spirits, Spooks, & Poltergeists

Real ghost phenomena have been present since history has been recorded. The fascination comes from the natural curiosity about life after death. All religions contain references to ghosts, or human spirits that are without their bodies, and all cultures contain stories of ghosts.

As a ghost investigator you need to have a solid understanding of what ghosts are, terms used, the forms ghosts can take, how to find and collect evidence of ghosts, communicating with ghosts, and how to get rid of them. In order to remain objective, stick to perspectives that are universal, meaning that they can be applied to any person from any religion and any culture. This is not a simple task since your own personal biases can alter your perception.

What are ghosts?

When you encounter people who know that you do ghost investigations, you're going to be asked "What are ghosts?" It is one of the most common questions a ghost investigator gets asked. **Ghosts** are lingering spiritual energy of either intelligent or residual consciousness left to fulfill a specific purpose. It is important to understand the sections of the definition so everyone is on the same page, figuratively speaking.

"Spiritual Energy" is a broad term that refers to the actual composition of the ghost. Some people say "spiritual energy", some use other terms like "soul". "Spiritual energy" is generally more open to the variety of religions out there, while "soul" can open up the proverbial can of worms. "Intelligent Consciousness" and "Residual Consciousness" are two definitive terms. A ghost will either be intelligent or residual. This will be discussed in detail for further understanding. "Specific Purpose" refers to why the ghost is present. Sometimes they don't know they are dead, they might need closure, they might feel the need to protect an object or person, and sometimes they want to be living once again.

Terms & Connotations

Intelligent and Residual are the first basic terms you need to know for ghosts.

Intelligent — *Intelligent* refers to the spirit of a person is unattached from its body and hangs around on earth instead of going to the afterlife, wherever that may be. This type of spirit is just a real as you or I, but is sometimes confused, or simply, lost.

Residual — *Residual* refers to the thoughts and emotions of living people become imprinted on a place or object. These thoughts manifest themselves later in a visual form, almost like a movie that periodically loops. These hauntings are usually with little or no sound and there is usually little or no interaction with the living. One example would be seeing a legion of Roman soldiers marching down the street. Each individual soldier does not have its own soul; it's simply a mirage of something that happened there before.

Word choice is an issue that many people overlook. The word that you choose to use may offend or mean something different to your client.

Below is a list of terms and connotations for ghost investigators to use. Make the proper word choice when talking to your client.

Ghost – Very general term that is considered neutral.

Spirit – This term can be perceived as a religious term if used incorrectly.

Demon or Angel – Very religious terms. You can offend people with these terms unless you explain exactly what you mean.

Phantasm – This is Italian for "ghost". Due to the language barrier in America, this has started to have a slight negative connation to it and it generally refers to a mischievous ghost.

Shade – This is an older term that is not often used. It usually denotes a non-threatening ghost who often issues a warning or is a bad omen.

Spook – A neutral sophomoric term.

Spectre – This term while meaning "ghost" often refers to full body or full torso apparitions.

Apparition – A general term that is very neutral. It refers to the physical and visual nature of the ghost, or what you can see, hear, smell, touch, etc.

Poltergeist – In German this means "noisy ghost". It has negative connotations and refers to a noisy and very active ghost.

Phantom – This has connotations of being a hoax due to the numerous amounts of mystery novels about mysterious phantoms.

Forms

There are only a handful of different forms that ghosts will take on. Provided are the names with descriptions and information.

Orbs – One of the most common forms of ghosts. The shape of an orb, a sphere, is a very common formation in nature like bubbles, many seeds, eyeballs, planets, etc. Orbs are spiritual energy from organic matter which includes plants, animals, birds, fish, and people. Orbs cannot be seen by the naked eye. Often times dust, insects, double images of the moon, water droplets, lights, and air particulates can be mistaken for orbs. Photographs taken in rapid succession of each other can successfully show orbs traveling through the photos.

Ledwith, Miceal and Klaus Heinemann. *The Orb Project.* Atria Books: New York, 2007.

Apparition – An apparition is a physical ghost usually that one usually sees, though smell, touch, hearing, and tastes are other factors that may present themselves. There are three types of apparitions: *dismembered parts, full torso,* and *full body. Dismembered parts* refers to any extremity that is not attached to a body like a pair of feet or just a head or even just a voice. *Full torso* refers to the area from the shoulders to the knees. *Full body* refers to an apparition that appears nearly or fully head to foot. Apparitions can appear as solid as any living person or creature, but they can also appear as a misty substance. A good example of this would be the famous 1936 photograph of the Brown Lady of Ranyham Hall taken by Captain Hubert C. Provand.

Bayless, Raymond. *Apparitions and Survival of Death.* University Books: New York, 1973.

Anecdote

When I first met the paranormal investigators from IOPIA, an Anchorage-based group in Alaska, they had come up to Fairbanks for two ghost investigations. As it happened, we ended up talking about ghost forms, especially orbs and apparitions. Neelie and Tony, the two investigators from IOPIA, and I found that orbs were our number one photographed anomaly and that we were all hoping for an apparition or vortex or anything else to appear. As it happened, after our trip up to Birch Hill Cemetery, where they had never been before, we had gathered an EVP (by Neelie) and a photo of an apparition (by myself) both at the same period of time. The apparition, a full torso apparition, is clearly set in front of some birch trees, next to some graves. When I took this picture, Neelie had captured a male voice saying "Helen" on her equipment after asking "Who is the lady in white?" As it happened, I was standing near the grave of Helen Findley. After some heavy research, including an order to the department of vital statistics for a death certificate, I determined that Helen Findley is Birch Hill Cemetery's *Lady in White*.

Poltergeist – A poltergeist may or may not have a physical body. It is however a malicious, noisy entity that is very often attached to a particular person or object. These ghosts have a bad reputation because they usually earn a bad reputation. Poltergeist have been the subject of a lot of modern research into the spirit realm, strongly starting in the 18th century, and have grown to become antagonists in modern day culture such as in the film *Poltergeist*.

Poltergeists can be a nuisance in a practical jokester way and they can also be very violent and aggressive. Poltergeists never appear to the naked eye, though on film or in photos they can appear as a large ball of energy, an orb, or as a misty substance. Poltergeists tend to focus on a select few individuals rather than effecting random people. They will do everything from move objects around, levitate people, scratch or slap people, irritate animals, make disruptive noises, flicker lights, disturb electronics, and create temperature differences.

Wilson, Colin. *Poltergeist! A Study in Destructive Haunting.* G.P. Putnam's Sons: New York, 1982.

Wraith – When a person sees a wraith, it is of a living person who will soon die. A person who claims to have seen a ghost of their self should be cautioned against their immediate plans. A famous case is that of poet Percy Shelley who saw his own wraith aboard the ship that would later be hit by a storm, leaving Shelley to drown in the Bay of Spezia.

Ghost Lights – There are many names for ghost lights such as St.Elmo's Fire and Will O' The Wisp. Ghost lights are caused by many things including ball lightning, swamp gas, glowing insects, and man-made objects like lights or reflective items. Ghost lights are notoriously hard to get close to. According to Dom. Augustin Calmet, these lights are simply "inflamed vapour".[4]

Vortex – A vortex is almost never visible to the naked eye. It's often a swirled, misty white object in a photograph. It has been theorized that a vortex is a doorway between the world of the living and the world of the dead.

---

[4] Calmet, *Dissertations Upon The Apparitions of Angels, Daemons, and Ghosts, and Concerning the Vampires of Hungary, Bohemia, Moravia, and Silesia (* ECCO Printing: London, 2010. Reprint of M. Cooper, 1759 edition.), 62.

Daimon/Daemon – *Daimon* (pron. "d-ay-muhn") is a Greek term that means "divine power". These spirits are synonymous with "Angel" or "Demon" which means that there are good daimons and bad daimons. It is important to use the term *Daimon* instead of *Angel* or *Demon* since you can easily offend someone by the other terms, and most people will automatically think you are a religious nut if you use strong religious terms. These spirits like to meddle with the living. It can range from friendly to mischievous to violent and aggressive. There are cases of bad daimons raping and/or physically abusing the living. The good daimons might appear before a person and deliver a warning or perhaps assist in saving a person's life.

Spirit Guides – Spirit guides are not ghosts. They are spiritual beings who exist on a wholly different plane of existence. Sometimes they are referred to as Guardian Angels or a guiding light. They can be mistaken for religious entities.

Brennan, Barbara. *Hands of Light: A Guide to Healing Through the Human Energy Field*. Bantam Books: New York, 1988.

Brennan, Barbara. *Light Emerging: The Journey of Personal Healing*. Bantam Books: New York, December 1993.

Shadow People – Shadow people are another type of entity that aren't ghosts. They are other-dimensional beings. Shadow people appear as living shadows. They often have no distinguishing features, except for their outline or form. They are grey to black in color and move independently of any present light source. Unlike a shadow that needs to have a light source and a surface to be seen on, shadow people can move throughout rooms, forests, parks, yards, houses, buildings, and anywhere else that you are able to move around in. Sometimes they seem to be observing humans, sometimes they become aggressive and violent, and sometimes you just see them moving around without any care towards humans.

There isn't a definitive way to permanently rid a house of shadow people. There are some ways of temporarily ridding a house of them and, sometimes, it can lead to a permanent fix. The person who is suffering from an infestation needs to command them to leave, if that doesn't work, there are reports of people praying, using house cleansing/blessing spells and rituals, and some people have actually turned their fear into anger, punching at the shadow people.[5] Out of these methods, the house cleansing/blessing rituals or spells seem most effective and can be done by anyone including any religious figure.

> Offutt, Jason. *Darkness Walks: The Shadow People Among Us*
> Anomalist Books: San Antonio, 2009.

Descriptors

Smells—Unexplainable scents often develop out of nowhere. These scents are often associated with who the ghost was while alive or where their lost bodies, if they happen to be lost, may be found. Common scents include: perfume/cologne, tobacco smoke, floral scents, and foul odors.

Sounds—Ghosts are known to knock on walls or bang on other objects. This activity could be part of a routine from their life, but could also be an attempt at contacting, or scaring the living. Likewise, disembodied voices or whispering are also common.

Cold spots—Often an area will become unexplainably cold. The theory surrounding this phenomenon is that a ghost

---

[5] Offutt, *Darkness Walks: The Shadow People Among Us* (Anomalist Books: San Antonio, 2009), 183-195.

requires a tremendous amount of energy when they manifest, to the point of even pulling heat out of the surrounding air.

Visual appearance—The visual appearance of a ghost, as a descriptor, is how the ghosts look when they do appear. It's important to note the color, the solidity, and the form they take on. Some ghosts look very human, but their feet may be a misty mass. Some ghosts are translucent white mists that form a human outline.

Air movement—Haunted places often feature sudden unexplainable gusts of air or wind that blow through rooms and past occupants.

Actions – Some ghosts do nothing more than repeat themselves over and over again, like a piece of video that is looped. These ghosts are called *repeaters*. Residual and intelligent ghosts are both capable of being repeaters. Other ghosts are considered *free-roaming*, a term that grew in popularity due to the film *Ghostbusters*. Free-roaming ghosts are simply not repeaters; they have the ability to wander around.

Actions also may include any particular action around an object, a person, a certain place, or at a certain time. You may very well have a free-roaming ghosts that has to knock on a certain wall, randomly, when they are seen passing it.

Evidence of Ghosts

Modern ghost investigators use a variety of equipment to detect spirits as shown in Chapter 2. As popularity in the field grows, the number of devices increases and the precision of that equipment improve as well. However, the presence of a ghost is known to interfere with proper functioning of electronic equipment. Investigators often view this interference as evidence itself.

The following are typical types readings collected by ghost investigators. You will find tips on what to look for and how to distinguish *prime evidence* from *garbage evidence*.

Prime evidence is evidence that is clear beyond a doubt to be unexplained. For instance, this could be a clear female voice saying "Hello" or a video recording of doors opening and closing with no assistance.

Garbage evidence is collected material that is questionable. For instance, this could be a garbled voice that sounds like it could be saying "forever" or "whatever" or "the river", but you aren't sure.

Sound Recording

When you are recording sound, begin every track with the location, time, date and the names of the investigators. Recording sound in haunted places can yield low level sounds. Investigators look for voices, growls, moans, sounds that are not present, and sounds that are present. Collecting voices on a voice recorder type of evidence is known as **Electronic Voice Phenomena (EVP).** Sound recording devices include tape recorders, microphones, digital recorders, laptops and other devices.

Going back through your tape or audio tracks, increase the volume. You may find very low recorded sound otherwise missed at normal volume levels. When you are making logs of any evidence found, be sure to mark the time down from the audio track. This may appear as 01:35:24.5 to 01:39:46.9, using the format of hour:minutes:seconds. You will also want to write down what was said and if you think it's Prime or Garbage evidence. Two standard entries will look something like this:

01:25:30.4	Female voice. Young. Sounds afraid.
To	"Check in the parlor."
01:34:04.9	5 seconds of silence.

	"He always goes to the parlor." Sound of heavy dragging. **Prime.**
01:46:07.4 To 01:49:03.5	Sound of distant door slamming shut. Could be from Team 2. Check on this. Currently: **Garbage**.

Collect the segments and play them back for your group. Ask for any interpretations. It is best not to inform them of what you wrote down in your entry in order to keep it unbiased. A solid prime piece of evidence will prove itself by being consistently heard.

Allow the others to listen to your garbage evidence as well. You may have something that is questionable to you, but coincides with another piece of evidence, making it actually prime evidence.

Save your segments, preferably with at least 2 seconds of lead and end time for your research files.

Markowitz, Mike. *EVP: Electronic Voice Phenomenon*. Schiffer Publishing: 2009.

Temperature Recording

A sudden change in ambient temperature can announce a ghost's presence, a thermometer can record that change. While investigating, keep track of how the temperature changes in an area. Thermometers come in a variety of shapes and sizes. Another common ghost investigation tool is a digital thermometer that detects temperature on the surface of an object from a distance.

When looking for temperature changes, you will definitely want to mark down the time and duration of any changes found. These changes will have to be compared to other evidence. You will also have to be aware that drafts,

THE PROFESSIONAL GHOST INVESTIGATOR

heating units, electronics, and steam can all alter the temperature in their areas.

Standard temperature entries will look like this:

Ambient Room Temperature   68F From 11:35pm to 11:36pm the temperature near the bedroom door dropped to 40F. Air conditioner is off.

Visual Recording

A camera, video or still, is essential to capturing visual activity. While it is a popular method in the television industry to hand-carry a video camera, it is preferred among professionals to stabilize the video camera by using a stationary tripod. By hand-carrying a video camera your film can be compromised by sudden or unnecessary movement. It is preferred, however, to carry a still camera for photography purposes.

For video purposes, it is best to set up your camera to run as long as possible without interruption to the recording. It is recommended that extra batteries be kept on hand, as well as extra video tape, storage discs, or film.

When looking back through video footage, you will want to record notes of when occurrences happen on film, much like you would for audio tracks, with the format hour:minutes:seconds. Here is an example:

02:15:30.4 To 02:17:45.4	Hallway door opens and closes. Sound of footsteps away from camera.
02:50:30.0 To 02:58:48.9	Rocking chair in the corner of living room rocks for 8 minutes.

For still camera photographs, you will want to mark down the digital file name or the number associated with the photo print, where it was taken, what to look for, and any additional information. Here is an example:

DSC0001.jpg DSC0002.jpg DSC0003.jpg DSC0004.jpg	Hallway. Four consecutive photographs of vaporous apparition in the form of a shrouded figure. Moves from the doorway to the window. Promptly vanishes. Did not see with the naked eye. **Prime**.
DSC0011.jpg DSC0012.jpg	Two orbs near living room window. Slight hexagon shape and fuzziness. Nothing seen with naked eye. Currently: **Garbage**.

Thermal Imaging

A thermal imager is a special camera that detects the amount of heat on the surface of an object. Spirits, or evidence of spirits, is known to show up as a temperature change. Thermal imaging technology can come as a still camera or a video camera of varying capability.

Electromagnetic Field Recording

Electromagnetic field detectors track how a field changes. A moving electromagnetic field, or unexplainable high readings, can signify the presence of a ghost. Be wary of electric wiring, devices like breaker boxes or electronics, appliances, and other items that give off an electromagnetic field. If you are in charge of using an EMF detector during an investigation, then you need to search for the potential causes. Also be aware that exposure to high EMF can cause a variety of physical symptoms, including headache, nausea, hallucination, nervousness and the feeling of being watched. When investigating, always record a 'base value' for the area. Note any significant change from this value, preferably done on a map of the area with small explanations. For example:

After making a baseline map, you can consider any high readings around previous marked high-level areas as Garbage evidence. Anything else out of the ordinary, you can mark as Prime. Be sure to have multiple copies of your original unmarked map, so you can take a fresh unmarked map on your investigation.

Animals & Children

It has been noted by many expert ghost investigators that children and animals are more inclined to sense and be affected by ghosts. Children may converse freely with a ghost, while the parent is fully unaware of its presence. Often times the parents believe that their child has an imaginary friend. This close bond can cause the child to suffer highly emotional reactions, violent behavior, or even just a change in behavior.

Animals can also be affected by ghosts. House pets may watch, bark/hiss, or run away from something in a room. There have been cases of animals becoming ill and even dying from ghost activity. Be sure to watch for a change in animal behavior.

Spiritual Communication

Spiritual communication is the communication between the living and the dead. There are a few good ways to proceed with this and few bad ways to go about it. First off, I am going to recommend checking out:

Buckland, Raymond. *Buckland's Book of Spirit Communications*. Llewellyn Publications: St.Paul, 2004. Third edition.

Buckland's book will give you step by step instructions on spiritual communication and provides great explanations.

Spiritualism n. The belief that the dead survive as spirits that can communicate with the living.[1]

The spiritual communication methods outlined in this book are based on the 19th century development of spiritualism. It does not mention methods based on witchcraft, religious means, or by folk culture methods. The five methods that you should absolutely know are: 1. Séance, 2. Automatic Writing, 3. Talking Boards, 4. Mediumship vs Channeling vs Possession, and 5. Trance Work.

Before you start any of these methods of spiritual communication, you should finish this chapter. Be sure that you are familiar with a handful of methods of *Spiritual Safety*.

Séance

A séance is an activity conducted by two or more people, one being the medium[6], which allows spirits to speak/act/guide through the medium until the medium cuts the connection. During a séance the medium retains full control over the spiritual connection, essentially acting as a door keeper. You can also think of a séance like a telephone conversation. You want to make a call to a foreign country, but you just don't know the phone number to dial. The medium is able to locate the phone number, make the call, and translate the message to you.

A séance will usually start with those involved sitting in a circle, often holding hands. The lights should be dim, perhaps with a lamp or a few candles lit to help the medium focus. The group will be asked by the medium to focus on who they want to communicate with. The medium will focus and connect to the spirit world. The more experienced the medium, the better chance you have to connect with the right spirit the first time.

---

[6] See Chapter 4 on Psychics for a further explanation.

Once the medium connects with the spirit realm, questions can be asked. At this time, while the medium is allowing the spirit to communicate through their body, things may move around the room, sounds may be heard, smells detected, and sitters may feel ghostly touches. The sitters should be aware of this beforehand, so they try not to break the circle. Let the medium instruct you when to break the circle.

Reading into the history of séances can bring up negative feelings towards the practice of séance. There were, and still are, many people out to scam others for money. You will come across stories of charlatans if you read further into this subject.

Example Of A Séance In Pop Culture

In the film *Beetlejuice,* the Deetz family and some of their friends decide to put on a séance towards the end of the film. They want to physically meet the ghosts who live in the attic. Otto, the one who leads the séance, reads certain passages from *The Handbook For The Recently Deceased* and instantly the two ghosts start to take on a physical form in center of the séance. Unfortunately, Otto was not a very good séance leader because he has no idea how to stop what he has started. Be sure that you have a full plan and that you know your spiritual safety.

Automatic Writing

Automatic writing is the act of unconsciously writing something. Essentially a spirit will move your arm and hand so a written piece is produced. Many who are capable of automatic writing sit and have sessions where they actively allow automatic writing to occur. The other people who are capable usually do not realize that they are or have written something down.

Many people who want to practice automatic writing will start by sitting in a comfortable spot with a pad of paper and a pencil. They start by asking if anyone would like to communicate with them. Often times they start by moving the pencil in a circle, waiting for the spirits to take over. It works best if the person has their attention focused elsewhere then their pad of paper.

This method takes time to develop, though there are those who are natural automatic writers like Elsa Barker. Elsa Barker of London began to receive letters from the deceased Judge David Patterson Hatch. She published the collection in 1914. Her work was published again in 1995 and in 2004.[7] Elsa was one of the many who was not aware of the communication until after it was done.

Example Of Automatic Writing In Pop Culture

Two examples immediately come to mind. On an episode of *X-Files*, Agent Mulder sees the spirit of his dead mother. When he looks down, after she disappears, he finds a note that she left for him through automatic writing.

The second example would be in the made-for-TV movie *Rose Red* one of the psychics in the group that visits the mansion Rose Red is an automatic writer.

Talking Boards

Talking boards are also called "Ouija boards" or "witch boards" and are considered a very dangerous tool. This is similar to having a séance, but only one person is needed. The board which has letters A-Z, numbers 0-9, Hello, Good-bye,

---

[7] Hatch, David Patterson. *Letters From The Afterlife*. Channeled by Elsa Barker. Beyond Words Publishing: Oregon, 2004.

Yes, and No across it and a planchette, otherwise known as a pointer.

Before going on, I want to caution against using any talking board. They eliminate the figure of the medium. This will leave you open to any spirit that comes along. Imagine being in a phone booth in a foreign country and you want to call your uncle who has just moved there. The phone book is four inches thick and you cannot read any of the words, so you pick up the phone, put in your quarter, and randomly start to dial a phone number. There is a definite loss of control when it comes to talking boards and there are lots of reports of negative communication.

Talking boards work by the one person, or multiple people, placing the planchette on the board and their fingertips lightly on the planchette. One person will ask a question and the group waits for a response. Another question is asked, another, and another. If spiritual communication takes place, the planchette will move around the board spelling out words. It is best to have someone not participating in holding the planchette to be a record keeper of any communication that comes through.

Example Of Talking Boards In Pop Culture

In *The Exorcist*, the young girl starts out by using an Ouija board. Things go horribly awry and she becomes possessed by the spirit she had been talking to through the Ouija board.

Mediumship vs Channeling vs Possession

There is a difference between mediumship, channeling, and possession. Mediums are able to make contact with spirits at will. They can relay messages to the living. When discussing séances, it was brought up that mediums are like telephones with their methods of contact. Mediums are often clairvoyant, they can "tune in" to spirits at any given time, and they can often pick and choose who to talk to.

Channeling is similar to mediumship as they can be looked upon as a telephone or direct conduit for spirits, but there are three distinct differences. Channelers usually have no sense of any type of clairvoyance abilities. They also typically have a select few, sometimes only one, spirit that they communicate with. Lastly, they can communicate with spirits and with those who have never lived on our physical plane. Those who have never lived on our physical plane are usually considered energy or light beings, elementals, and beings of other dimensions.

Brennan, Barbara. *Hands of Light: A Guide to Healing Through the Human Energy Field*. Bantam Books: New York, 1988.

Brennan, Barbara. *Light Emerging: The Journey of Personal Healing*. Bantam Books: New York, December 1993.

Possession is what occurs when a spirit takes over a person's body without their permission. This happens in every culture and every culture has a remedy for it. Possessions are dangerous and are not for the weak. Possessions can start out seemingly harmless. It might be a slight personality change, a mental disorder, or medical condition. The longer it continues, the stronger the spirit becomes until there is a full bodily take over.

Kiely, David M. and Christina McKenna. *The Dark Sacrament*. HarperOne: New York, 2007.

Example Of Mediums, Channeling, and Possession In Pop Culture

The little boy in *The Sixth Sense* is an example of a medium. He saw multiple dead people, he could converse with them, and he could pass messages along to the living.

In the 1993 film *Heart & Souls*, Robert Downey Jr. can

communicate with four spirits who act as his 'guardian angels'. He has no special powers, except for hearing his spirit guardians.

In *The Exorcist*, the character of Reagan went through various stages of possession until she was fully taken over by the daimon.

Trance Work

Trances are achievable by everyone with some practice. It's the change of brainwaves from beta, our normal state of mind, to either the alpha or theta state during a meditation. Some people can naturally put themselves in a trance state while others have to work at it. The more often it's practiced, the quicker it is to put yourself there. People use trances for energy work, spiritual communication, astral travelling, hypnosis, and for rituals.

A beginning exercise: Starting out, a person should find a quiet, comfortable place to sit. Sometimes non-lyrical music or nature sounds at a low volume can help people with trances. Close your eyes and visualize yourself on a path. The stronger the visualization, the stronger your trance. Walk along the path and look around you as you might do when you physically walk along a path. Eventually visualize the path leading you to a pool of water. Look at your reflection in the water. Remember what you see in the water. When you are ready think to yourself: "It's alright. I can wake up now." Drift away from the water. Drift back to the path. Drift back to consciousness.

It will also be beneficial to learn how to create a circle of protection around yourself. Visualize yourself as you are. Visualize a protective circle forming around yourself. It can be a circle of light, concrete, a system of roots and plants, ice, a bubble, or anything else that your mind comes up with. Tell yourself that you are protected and no person or thing can enter without your permission. It's recommended by nearly every author who talks about trances to create a protective circle around one's self before every trance session.

Mariechild, Diane. *Mother Wit*. The Crossing Press: California, 1987.

Getting Rid of Ghosts

The method of getting rid of ghosts is typically called "clearing" or "to clear an area". One method of **clearing**, is to perform a ritual, typically with chanting or by using herbs, that will return the area to a neutral state, a balanced and stable environment. Another method of clearing is using a removal practice. Removal practices are tied to religion and involve blessing an area, holy water, using a spirit-chasing stick, or other item. Lastly, some psychics can communicate with spirits directly, and help them to move on.

Threatening or forcing a spirit to move on is generally not recommended, but sometimes necessary depending on the case. Often, a ghost will need to be removed more than once for the effect to be permanent.

The three methods of removal require a strong-willed person and the proper tools. Instructions for each three methods are listed below. Attempt these before you attempt anything else. Other methods of ghost removal, for stronger spirits, will be listed later. Use one of these methods of clearing first.

Ritual Clearing

This particular ritual is based on many indigenous shamanic beliefs.

Needed:

- Matches or Lighter
- Sage Smudge-Stick
- Abalone Shell or Bird Wing or small handheld Fan

The person conducting the ritual will need to go into each room of the house during this ritual. The smudge-stick needs to be lit and left to smolder. Use the shell, wing, or small fan to direct the smoke and increase the smoldering. In each room, keep the windows closed, spread the smoke around the room. Spend extra time in the areas where the activity has been most prominent. In each room the person conducting the ritual needs to say, with firm authority, something to the effect that the spirits are not welcome and that they should leave. You can use the following as a general command.

> "Spirit, you are not welcome in this
> house. You are forbidden to be here.
> Leave and do not return."

Remember to be authoritative. It is best if the owner of the property is the person to conduct the ritual. Be sure to take your time. Make sure the person conducting the ritual stays focused. Allow the smoke to dissipate before opening any windows.

Herbs and plants that you can add to your sage that also assist in purifying an area are: the bark of the Birch tree, Mugwort, St.John's Wort, Wormwood, Bamboo, and Vervain.

Removal Practices

This particular spell comes from *The Encyclopedia of 5000 Spells* by Judika Illes. It is called the "New Home Major Cleansing Spell".

Needed:

- Frankincense and Sandalwood essential oils
- Olive Oil
- Small Blue Candle
- Sea Salt
- A Disposable Tablecloth or Newspaper

1. Blend the essential oils with the olive oil.
2. Use the oil mixture to dress the candle. Hold the wick and dip the candle in the oil mixture.
3. Place the candle onto a saucer or plate and place that on top of a disposable tablecloth or several newspapers taped together that you have spread out in a room.
4. Make a large circle with sea salt on the tablecloth or newspaper. Be sure you can step into the circle.
5. Enter the circle and light the candle. Do not leave the circle until the candle has burnt out. Focus on the home being cleansed.
6. When the candle is finished burning, fold up the tablecloth or newspapers. Do not spill any salt or any items used for the ritual. Take everything to a moving body of water far from your home and dump the biodegradable items. The rest can be thrown away in a trash can far from your home.
7. Repeat in every room you need cleansed.

Psychic Assistance

Psychics can assist you in a variety of ways; the most common form is through that of a medium. It is difficult to give you proper directions with psychic assistance, but I can give you some generalities and guidelines.

A psychic that is prepared to help you will tell you how they communicate with spirits. They can help with strongly asking the spirit to leave. They can also assist with the stronger spirits, but you might leave them as a last resort.

Be sure to read Chapter 4 on psychics to learn why you might need a psychic, what to look for in a psychic, and the types of psychics. You might have one kind of psychic available and they may be wrong for the job. Be sure to check out your psychic before you employ their assistance.

It goes without saying that there are more ways out there to remove ghosts. One alternative method of dealing with a ghost is to get a family member with a strong tie to the ghost to demand the spirit to leave. Do some research and find ways that you feel comfortable with. If you are comfortable with them, chances are your clients will be comfortable with them.

Stronger spirits who won't leave may require you to seek assistance from a priest, a witch, a shaman, or a strong psychic. This means that you alone cannot handle the ghost problem which is fine. Have the person you seek assistance from perform a blessing first. This is usually a house blessing or a protective blessing of some kind. If that doesn't work, ask them what they recommend next. Many times a blessing from a spiritual authority, like a priest, is enough to get rid of the stronger spirits.

On occasion you may find that you will need to help the ghost solve their unfinished business, in which case you will require the assistance of a psychic.

Assistance of Unfinished Business

Everyone's unfinished business is different. Taking on a case where you find it necessary to assist with unfinished business is much like being a private investigator. Your goal is to find out what the spirit wants and then to give it to them. Sometimes it is as simple as finding a family member or a death notice of a loved one. Other times it becomes more complicated.

The spirits who need assistance are typically the non-violent ghosts, both intelligent and residual. There are many stories of ghosts traveling an old road where a bone went missing or of women waiting for their soldier husbands to return home from war. These are the easily recognizable cases. If you find the bone of the traveling spirit on the old road and bury it with the rest of his bones, he may very well be at peace. The woman waiting for her husband needs to know what became of her husband.

With the ghost of the woman waiting for her husband, you may need to ask a psychic to communicate with the spirit. Find out what happened with the husband and have a copy of an official document for the spirit. The psychic may be able to direct the spirit to the document.

Be prepared for this not to work for every case. Also, be prepared for long hours spent doing research.

Spiritual Safety

When you deal with ghosts, you're dealing with the spiritual realm. It is best to have protection which is actually a fairly simple process. Just keep in mind: *You Have The Final Say Over Your Self And Bad Spiritual Energy Can Only Attach*

Itself If You Allow It. You can use a **Circle of Protection**, previously mentioned in Trance Work in this chapter. It is recommended universally to use white or blue coloring in your protective circle.

Salt is a universal protector throughout the cultures of the world. Since ancient times salt has been used for spells, rituals, protection, and purification. If you feel threatened, you can stand in a ring of salt and be protected from any spiritual danger. As a side note, you may use half a box of salt on just a personal circle. You might want a second box of salt on hand for a dangerous case.

After you are done with a case, you want to make sure that you don't accidentally bring something home with you. You can simply verbally demand that you do not allow spirits to attach themselves to you or to follow you. You can again use a Circle of Protection, imagining a white or blue coloring in your protective circle. You can even go home and take a salt bath. I recommend 2-3 cups of Epsom salt for a standard bathtub to get the proper salinity.

This is a subject that is easy to research. You can look into crystals, witchcraft, religious protection, how various cultures protect themselves, folklore, etc. Use the method that is comfortable for you to use.

Possessions & Exorcisms

Possessions and exorcisms are last resorts. Too many amateurs want to jump to conclusions and claim a possession and/or an exorcism. A **possession** is what occurs when a spirit(s) takes over a person's body without their permission. An **exorcism** is a ritual used to remove the spirit from the possessed person. It is important to note that an exorcism does not always work, is a ritual in every religion and culture, is highly dangerous, and should only be a last resort.

It is important to look into the various religions and cultures in order to see their practices on exorcism. Below are a handful of different methods of exorcisms. You will need to do research on your client's religion before you even attempt to declare an exorcism.

The **Catholics**, possibly the most famous for their exorcisms, use chapter 13 of the text *The Roman Ritual* for their rites.

Hindus use *yajnas*, a ritual sacrifice and burning of herbs, and the text *Garuda Purana*.

In **Islam**, exorcisms are called *ruqya*. There are various parts of the Qur'an used, but most commonly used are the last three suras: Surat al-Ikhlas (The Fidelity), Surat al-Falaq (The Dawn), and Surat al-Nas (Mankind).

Judaism uses a rabbi and a team of ten called the *minyan*. They use Psalm 91 and, the rabbi only, uses a ram's horn to make sounds that will "shatter the body", forcing the possessing spirit to leave.

Maori call exorcisms *mākutu lifting*, *mākutu* meaning "witchcraft, sorcery". It involves ritual chanting and drumming, among other rites that only *tohunga*, Maori priests, are supposed to know.

Pentecostal and other deliverance ministries "cast out" possessing spirits all the time. Deliverance, which is what this is usually called, is not quite a full-blown exorcism, but can be considered a light exorcism.

Daoist priests use a text called the *Daozang* which has three parts to it, the last part being on exorcisms. Daoists often use talismans.

Shamans of various indigenous peoples around the world often use medicine songs and chants to rid a person of possessing spirits.

Practitioners of **witchcraft** have many rituals, sacrifices, chants, and methods for being rid of possessing spirits. Be aware that there are many types of witchcraft and some do not accept the ways of others.

If you decide that your client is indeed possessed, you need to have proof to show to the priest/minister/shaman/witch that will assist in the ritual needed to free your client of the possessing spirit. The Catholics have a list of common occurrences with people in need of an exorcism. I suggest using the list as a guide to help you distinguish the possessed from the people who may just need psychological or medical help. This recommendation is made because the Catholics have the major signs of possession listed. It's not due to a religious or cultural bias.

Catholic Signs of Possession

1. Lack of appetite.
2. Cutting, scratching, and biting of skin.
3. A cold feeling in the room.
4. Unnatural bodily postures.
5. A change in the person's voice.
6. Supernatural strength not subject to that person's gender or age.
7. The possessed speaks in another language which they had never learned before.
8. Violent rejection toward all religious objects or items.

If you decide that you may have a possessed person to deal with, your first step will be to collect evidence. Obtain photos, video, audio recordings, and whatever other evidence you come across. Ask the family or guardian of the possessed person about their religious affiliations. If they are of no religious affiliation, ask if they would be willing to use a particular church or other group to assist in clearing up their possession issue.

Call or visit the church or group that your client is affiliated with. Present your case as a "possible possession" and have a copy of your evidence ready for showing. It's best to leave a copy of evidence with the church so they can review it and get back to you. Be sure to leave them your contact information, your client's name, and the victim's name. Have the priest call you to let you know if they will help or not.

You should be extremely discrete when it comes to discussing the case with anyone. Be aware of how it will affect people, especially of the friends and family members of the victim. Do not bring the media into the situation.

If you do get assistance from a church or group, allow them to take over the actual exorcism process. You can resume being in charge after they are finished. During their exorcism, you can collect data if they allow it, but do not interfere unless asked.

Chapter 3 Quiz

Define

Ghost

Prime Evidence

Garbage Evidence

Electronic Voice Phenomena (EVP)

Cold Spot

Mediums

Channeling

Possession

Questions

1. What is the difference between an Intelligent ghost and a Residual ghost?

2. What are the connotations for the terms: ghost, phantasm, shade, apparition, spook, poltergeist, and demon/angel?

3. What are the 9 forms that ghosts take on?

4. What are the 5 methods of spiritual communication that every ghost investigator should know?

5. What is *clearing* and how can it be accomplished?

6. What is spiritual safety?

7. What is the first step for dealing with a supposed possession?

Chapter 4 – Psychics

Psychics, in a nutshell, are people who can gather information through some means of **extra sensory perception (ESP)**. ESP is an extension of our regular senses, but more so. Those who use ESP can reach out with a type of sixth sense to gather information not available or not easily obtainable. You may also come across the term **psi** which, according to the Parapsychological Association, means it is "used either as a noun or adjective to identify paranormal processes and paranormal causation; the two main categories of psi are psi-gamma (paranormal cognition; extrasensory perception) and psi-kappa (paranormal action; psychokinesis), although the purpose of the term "psi" is to suggest that they might simply be different aspects of a single process, rather than distinct and essentially different processes."[8] ESP is broken up into two categories: **Telepathy** and **Clairvoyance**.

Telepathy is the transfer of information on thoughts or feelings between individuals by means other than the five senses. A person who is able to make use of telepathy is said to be able to read the thoughts and stored information in the brain of others. There are four types of telepathy.

Types of Telepathy
1. **Latent Telepathy**, formerly known as "*deferred telepathy*", is described as being the transfer of

---

[8] "Psi., definition" Parapsychological Association. 1997-2012. http://www.parapsych.org/

information, through Psi, with an observable time-lag between transmission and receipt.

2. **Retrocognitive, Precognitive, and Intuitive Telepathy** is described as being the transfer of information, through Psi, about the past, future or present state of an individual's mind.

3. **Emotive Telepathy**, also known as remote influence or emotional transfer, is the process of transferring kinesthetic sensations through altered states.

4. **Superconscious Telepathy**, involves tapping into the superconscious to access the collective wisdom of the human species for knowledge.

   - **Telekinetics** - The term psychokinesis, also known as telekinesis, sometimes abbreviated PK and TK respectively, is a term coined by publisher Henry Holt to refer to the direct influence of mind on a physical system that cannot be entirely accounted for by the mediation of any known physical energy. Examples of psychokinesis could include distorting or moving an object, and influencing the output of a random number generator.

   - **Precognition** - Precognition, also called Future Sight, refers to perception that involves the acquisition of future information that cannot be deduced from presently available and normally acquired sense-based information. A related term, presentiment, refers to information about future events that is perceived as emotions. The terms are usually used to denote a seemingly parapsychological or extrasensory process of perception, including clairvoyance.

Retrocognition - Frederic W. H. Myers coined the term *retrocognition* (also known as postcognition) and describes it as "knowledge of a past event which could not have been learned or inferred by normal means". Retrocognition has long been held by scientific researchers into psychic phenomena to be untestable, given that, in order to verify that an accurate retrocognitive experience has occurred, it is necessary to consult existing documents and human knowledge, the existence of which permits some contemporary basis of the knowledge to be raised.

Clairvoyance is the ability to clearly see, in the mind's eye, an event or image in the past, present, or future. Most of the time what is seen is a brief image or symbol; sometimes it may come in the form of short clips as if taken from a film. There are five main types of clairvoyants.

- **Clairsentience (feeling/touching)** - In the field of parapsychology, clairsentience is a form of extra-sensory perception wherein a person acquires psychic knowledge primarily by means of feeling. **Psychometry**, the acquisition of knowledge by physically touching an item or person, is related to clairsentience. The word stems from *psyche* and *metric*, which means "to measure with the mind".

- **Clairaudience (hearing/listening)** - In the field of parapsychology, clairaudience is a form of extra-sensory perception wherein a person acquires information by paranormal auditory means. Clairaudience is essentially the ability to hear in a paranormal manner, as opposed to paranormal seeing (clairvoyance) and feeling (clairsentience). Clairaudient people have psi-mediated hearing. Clairaudience may refer, not to actual perception of sound, but may instead indicate impressions of the "inner mental ear" similar to the way many people think words without having auditory impressions. But it may also refer to actual perception of sounds such as voices, tones, or noises which are not apparent to other humans or to recording equipment.

- **Clairalience (smelling)** - Also known as *Clairescence*. In the field of parapsychology, clairalience is a form of extra-sensory perception wherein a person acquires psychic knowledge primarily by means of smelling.

- **Claircognizance (knowing)** - In the field of parapsychology, claircognizance is a form of extra-sensory perception wherein a person acquires psychic knowledge primarily by means of intrinsic knowledge. It is the ability to know something without a physical explanation why you know it, like the concept of mediums.

- **Clairgustance (tasting)** - In the field of parapsychology, clairgustance is defined as a form of extra-sensory perception that allegedly allows one to taste a substance without putting anything in one's mouth. It is claimed that those who possess this ability are able to perceive the essence of a substance from the spiritual or ethereal realms through taste.

Ghost Investigators & Psychics

True psychics are very useful for ghost investigators since they provide a direct spiritual connection. Psychics can also provide clues for cases from where an incident occurred to what the spirits are looking for to keywords to search for while doing your research. Psychics also may require some help testing their abilities.

This is where parapsychology starts to come into play with ghost investigations. **Parapsychology** is the study of psychical research and originally started with mesmerism in the late-18th Century. Modern-day parapsychologists study ESP, PK, poltergeists, paranormal photography, sleep and dreams, altered states of consciousness, psychic healing, psychopathology, reincarnation, death survival, and the relation of parapsychology with other fields of work.

A Case of Parapsychology in Pop Culture
In the film *Ghostbusters*, Dr.Peter Venkman was a psychologist and parapsychologist. To most people who didn't read between the lines, Venkman was a goofy guy who was pretty good with the one-liners. Those of you who looked closer at what he had been doing in the beginning of the film, his experiment; you'll notice that he was actually working – despite his flirting with the blonde. His experiment was: "The study of the effect of negative reinforcement upon ESP ability". The blonde was his control subject and the guy was his actual test subject.

Handbook of Parapsychology. Benjamin B. Wolman, ed. Van Nostrand Reinhold: New York, 1977.

Broughton PhD, Richard S. *Parapsychology: The Controversial Science*. Ballantine Books: New York, 1991.

There are a lot of phonies in the psychic world, as you probably already know. There are a lot of people out there with minimal abilities as well. Psychics with strong abilities are usually somewhat hard to find. It's recommended that when you do find a psychic, you ask to test them.

Anecdote

During my time with PEAK, after going through our new business and old business, we would do group workshops. Many of these were what we call "Psychic Games". We would develop our own test and run through it with the group. Sometimes it required everyone bringing in a small object in a box or bag so no one could see it. Sometimes it was an attempt to run through creating a psychic shield, which is a part of spiritual protection. Sometimes it was something kind of silly such as writing a common name, thing, or place on an index card, concentrating on it, and having the group guess what was on the card.

These "psychic games" helped us out with understanding psychic activity, having a familiarity with devising and using tests for psychic activity, and it also provided us with the knowledge of who in the group was potentially psychic. As it turned out we had a full range of people. Some were quick and quite accurate at picking things up that they were able to touch. Others could barely pick up anything. Some folks were better with getting readings from actual people, instead of objects. Some folks were better at getting a past signature on objects, then getting any kind of reading of the present or future.

There are five things that I learned from starting the "psychic games". 1. If you are ever in need of an activity for a meeting, try a psychic game. 2. Even the people who seem to have no ability can gradually gain ability, and psychic games are a good way for them to practice. 3. This is a great way to teach your team about spiritual protection. 4. Even a group talk about psychic games is a great way to get ideas for future games. 5. Psychic games are just fun.

Testing Psychics

Testing a psychic means experiments, and experiments mean following the standard **scientific process**. What this means is that when you write up your paper, both before and after the experimentation, you will want to follow the format of: Characterizations/Observations, Hypothesis, Predictions, and Experiments. It's a very simple process that has been imbedded in our minds since elementary school. The goal is to find a conclusion that could be repeated in the future.

The investigation of a psychic event(s), which are highly individualistic and varied, is mainly done over a course of time while being face-to-face with the client(s). The investigation of a psychic event could be termed "the proving of a psychic". The goal is to determine the following:

1. The type of psychic the client is.
2. What their strengths and weaknesses are.
3. What their limits are, psychically speaking.
4. To assist them with progressing their abilities, if they so choose.

Typically, the client will have an idea, before they come to your team, about what kind of psychic they are. They might mention that they smelled something and just knew or they had a dream about a car accident and then they witnessed it happen the next day. The first priority is going to be determining the type of psychic that you're dealing with. Develop your own type of test for that particular type of psychic.

Testing requires that you follow the strict guidelines of science, otherwise you're wasting your time. Developing your own psychic test will require you to have a control subject and a test subject. You may have to repeat the test a number of times in order to get good final results or results that you can chart. When developing your test and hypothesis, you need to think about issues that may arise with the experiment like flaws or a weak hypothesis.

When determining tests to run for psychic ability testing, it may be best to research the particular type of psychic that your client is. There have been numerous books and journals published about psychic testing. The US, UK, Chinese, and Russian governments have all undergone, and still are undergoing, psychic research. There are some very basic testing techniques, such as the four popular methods following. Other techniques will have to be devised by the investigator. Remember to document everything.

Zener Cards

The twenty-five card deck, five copies of five symbols, is mainly used for telepathy and general clairvoyance. The test is performed with a tester, the client (test subject), and a non-psychic person (your control subject). The test subject and the control subject should not know anything about each other, except each other's names (it won't affect the results). Have both subjects sit across a table or desk from the tester. The tester should have the deck of zener cards shuffled, ready to go. Between the tester and the subjects should be an opaque screen of some sort to prevent the subjects from being able to visually see the zener cards. Starting with the deck face down behind the screen, the tester will pick the topmost card and look at the shape on the card. The tester will then ask the control subject what is on the card. The next card the tester will ask the test subject.

The process will repeat until the tester goes through the whole deck. Many times the tester will go through the deck two or three times before ending the testing, shuffling the cards between rounds. During the testing, the tester will make note of what card is drawn and what the responses from the subjects are. The subjects will not be shown any of the cards before or after the testing.

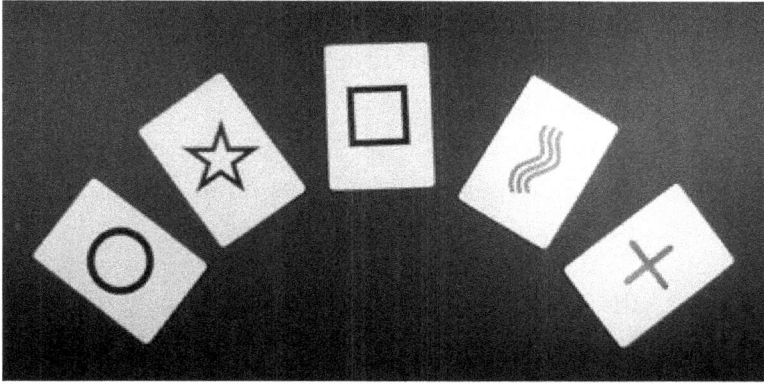

Your goal is to find someone with 80% accuracy or better. Other testing should follow if you do find a highly accurate psychic. Zener cards can lead to other testing, such as an "image vs. text" test or "what picture is in the envelope" or other such tests.

Psychometry Test

This is typically done with people who are clairsentient, claircognizance, and retrocognitive. This can be done with items inside bags or boxes, or it can be done with objects not in any containers. The idea is simple: What is the history or information associated with the item? The tester should find 25 to 50 items that they know the background of. The background of an item might include who it belonged to, any significance to the object, what the object was used for, etc.

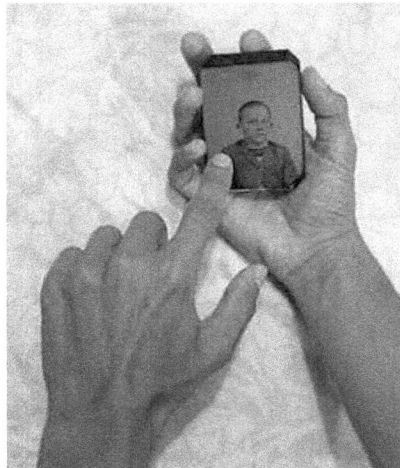

The objects should remain hidden from the client until the tester pulls one out. The tester will keep notes while the client tries to get a reading on the item in front of them. This means that they might have to touch the object.

Ganzfeld Experiment

A ganzfeld experiment is a technique used in the field of parapsychology to test individuals for extrasensory perception (ESP). It uses homogeneous and unpatterned sensory stimulation to produce an effect similar to sensory deprivation. The deprivation of patterned sensory input is 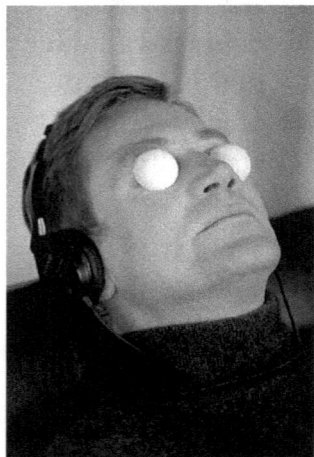 said to be conducive to inwardly generated impressions. In a typical ganzfeld experiment, a "receiver" is left in a room relaxing in a comfortable chair with halved Ping-Pong balls over the eyes, having a red light shone on them. The receiver also wears a set of headphones through which white or pink noise (static) is played. The receiver is in this state of mild sensory deprivation for half an hour. During this time a "sender" observes a randomly chosen target and tries to mentally send this information to the receiver. The receiver speaks out loud during the thirty minutes, describing what he or she can see. This is recorded by the experimenter (who is blind to the target) both by recording onto tape or by taking notes, and is used to help the receiver during the judging procedure. In the judging procedure, the receiver is taken out of the ganzfeld state and given a set of possible targets, from which they must decide which one most resembled the images they witnessed. Most commonly there are three decoys along with a copy of the target itself, giving an expected overall hit rate of 25% over several dozens of trials.

Random Number Generator

This is a test for those who claim to be psychokinetic (telekinetic). In the most common experiment of this type, a true random number generator (RNG), based on electronic or radioactive noise, produces a data stream that is recorded and analyzed by computer software. A subject attempts to mentally alter the distribution of the random numbers, usually in an experimental design that is functionally equivalent to getting more "heads" than "tails" while flipping a coin. In the RNG experiment, design flexibility can be combined with rigorous controls, while collecting a large amount of data in very short period of time. This technique has been used both to test individuals for psychokinesis and to test the possible influence on RNGs of large groups of people. Random number generators can be found online. This experiment can also be done with a bingo cage full of balls.

By going through numerous testing periods over a set amount of time, you should be able to determine some of the strengths and weaknesses are for your client. Some people may not be able to interpret color, while other might not be able to interpret other things. It may become evident that your client can easily read children while adults prove to be more difficult. This needs to be noted and experimented on. Once you have concluded your testing, which should leave you with a firm conclusion of your client's abilities; you will need to provide assistance for your client's progress.

Chapter 4 Quiz

Define

Extra Sensory Perception

Telepathy

Clairvoyance

Parapsychology

Questions

1. What are the 4 types of telepathy?
2. What are the 5 types of Clairvoyance?
3. What is the scientific process?
4. What are psychic games?
5. Why would someone want to use zener cards?
6. What is psychometry?
7. What is the ganzfeld experiment?
8. Who would benefit from a random number generator test?

Chapter 5 – Preliminary Investigations

Preliminary investigations are the core to any ghost investigation. It consists of the baseline information that you get from your client (initial information, witness statements, interviews, any preliminary photographs or other media) and initial research. You will need a strong preliminary investigation if you want to have a solid case.

Your baseline information starts once your initial information is presented. After you collect your baseline information you can move on to obtaining other witness statements, interviews, and progressing to research.

Activity Log

When you start your preliminary investigation, automatically have any investigator working on the case begin their own activity log. This is essentially a personal journal of what they are working on, sources they checked with the results, calls they make, etc. The activity log should be updated all the time for each case. The following is an example of a properly documented activity log.

3/5/2012

9:45 am

Called the witness Jane Lane on her cell phone, but received no answer. Left message asking her to call me. Promptly went on to review her three photos that she emailed. The photos were taken at the northwest corner of

---

Olive Hill Cemetery.

Photo 1: The three orbs in this photograph are all round with an inner glow. They are focused around an old tree in a clearing. The tree has a multitude of nails in the trunk. Witchcraft? Urban legend? Jane's friend, Amy is posing next to the tree.

Photo 2: Another picture of the tree from the same location. The orbs have moved and have gone from a white-yellow glow to a yellow-red glow. Amy is posing next to the tree.

10:25 am

Jane Lane called me back. Her initial reason for taking the pictures was "to take a few pictures of the nails in the trees. It was so weird, like something out of a horror novel or something." She said that the orbs were not seen when she took the photos. She only noticed them when she was going through them back home.

Set up a meeting with Jane Lane for tonight at 6pm at The Diner.

Photo 3: This picture has the three orbs close together near the branches of the tree with a vortex forming where the nails are on the tree. Amy has turned her head and has taken a step away from the tree.

5:45 pm

Leaving for The Diner. Meeting Jane Lane for an interview.

6:02 pm

Sitting at The Diner with Jane Lane. Recording the interview. See written transcript of interview for details.

The activity log needs to remain well documented. It will be your main reference for your final report. It will also help you keep things in order with your case, both mentally and physically with the paperwork.

Baseline Information

Baseline information is basic information about your case. This information is used to prevent investigators from going into a case "cold" (without information). Baseline information is always gathered from the witness(es) separately, otherwise you may end up with people talking over everyone else (muddled information).

Typically, whoever contacts you about the case, is interviewed first. You will learn about other witnesses and you can then pull other people aside to interview them at appropriate times. Sometimes with children, it's easier to have a parent to sit with them, but don't allow the parent to prevent the child from sharing. Make sure you always act professionally and be respectful of the person you are interviewing.

The most important questions to ask are your basic W's: **who**, **why**, **what**, **when**, and **where**. Tailor your questions to the situation. Recording the entire interview will ensure everything is captured and can be reviewed again. I recommend taking a voice recorder and just record the entire interview. That way you won't forget anything and it will make report writing easier. Start your recording with the time, the date, an audible title such as "Interview with John Doe", and the investigators who are present.

Here are some really basic questions that apply to most cases.

1. Can I get you to spell out your full name for me?
2. Can you tell me, *briefly*, what's been going on?
3. Who else was involved or affected?
4. Can you tell me *in more detail* what's been going on?
5. How long has this been going on?
6. Where has this been going on?
7. Do you have any idea why this might be going on?

8. Have you recently come into contact with anything that might have spurned this on?

9. Do you have any photos or video footage from the incident?

These questions are general in nature. Keep in mind that you want to keep the first three questions short. You want to know who they are (possibly what they do), a very brief explanation of what's going on, and who else is involved. If anything, this is the most important information because it gives us a clue as to what is going on.

Once you have your first three questions answered, it's time to indulge. Ask about what's been going on IN DETAIL, ask about the length of the incident, ask about location, and ask about anything that comes to mind. Religion should come into play if there's a suspected haunting. Finding out what religion someone belongs to will assist in trying to get the right kind of religious figure to help, if it's required. Obviously, a catholic would probably prefer a priest to a rabbi. This might also give us an idea on how the interviewee is dealing with things.

Interviewing the person(s) is not always the end of your baseline information. Conduct a video or a photographic walkthrough of the area under investigation. If a walkthrough is not possible, then ask for any photos, video, house/building layout, or any other sort of visual evidence when meeting to interview the witness. This is not always possible, but it really can help out an investigation.

Documentation allows investigators to know what sort of thing to look for, for a possible hoax, and it can give us a general idea of the layout of the area under investigation. Gather history, maps, photos, news articles, ghost information, property information, and anything else that you can think of. From here, you can move on to research.

Practice

While interviewing skills come natural to some, most people need a little practice before going out and obtaining baseline information. For a post-meeting workshop try practicing your interviewing skills.

1. Have everyone write out, ahead of time, three scenarios. Make sure they include a name, an incident in about 3 paragraphs, and a list of vital information that the interviewer should obtain from them that may or may not be directly in the incident paragraphs.

2. You can trade the scenarios around or have everyone keep their own. Just make sure that everyone pairs up for the activity, each with their own secret scenarios.

3. The interviewer starts, generally with "Hello, I'm [enter name here]. I am the initial investigator for your case. [etc]" The interviewer should try to obtain all the information possible from the "client" (the person with the scenario). The interviewer should take notes during the workshop.

4. The interviewee should not lead the investigator for information that is present on their scenario write-up. Try to act naturally and be ready to embellish on the scenario.

5. At the end, review the scenarios. Were there any problems that you had? Did you forget to ask certain questions? A group discussion about the interview process should end the workshop.

Initial Research

Research is the bulk of the ghost investigator's work. The general idea behind research is to collect information and data about your case. Your initial research is research based off of your collected baseline information. Refer to the research tools mentioned in chapter 2. This will give you a firm starting point for your future research.

Here are five example cases along with what you could research based off the cases.

Example 1:

"Repeatedly at my house, 224 Mountain Top Road, I have been seeing the figure of a man with a hatchet or an axe between 6pm and 9:30pm on a daily basis. I don't really see many details because he always seems to be covered in a shadow. I can tell he's a man by the shape of his body. I also have been hearing shrieks from the woods and sometimes the sound of footsteps both outside and inside the house. If I am alone, like when my dog is out in the yard and I'm inside, I have been slapped. The slapping started four days ago. I've checked with neighbors to see if they know anything about it, but the closest one is a half mile away and no one knows anything."

Look at the known facts about this case. We know that the client lives at 224 Mountain Top Road and that his nearest neighbor is a half mile away. Researching the location, previous owners and the history of the land, would be beneficial. There might have been a crime or an old Indian battle or even an old burial site in that area, unknown to the client. We also know that the man carries something hatchet or axe-like and that he shows up between 6pm and 9:30pm on a regular basis. This might be significant to a time of battle or a time of crime. The slapping seems to be a territorial or a claim of possession of the house/land made by the ghost. Once you figure out what might be going on, look through some old newspapers at your local library.

Example 2:

"A lady in white haunts the cemetery on the hill. A young boy is sometimes seen up there too in clothes from the '30s."

This is a typical blurb that you might find on a website or in a book about hauntings in your area. The first thing to do is to look at the history of the cemetery. Let's say that the cemetery was established in 1937. The young boy, if the observations are correct, would have been buried in the first few years of the cemetery opening up. You can probably find a list of possible young boys on a gravestone listing for the cemetery. The lady in white might be a little harder to pin point unless you figure out some additional information about her. Someone might have noticed the style of clothing she was in or where she was seen roaming around. You will also want to try to trace back the earliest known sightings and witnesses to known sightings.

Example 3:

"My wife and I retired three years ago. Six months ago we bought an old motel with 24 rooms, as a way to keep busy and make some extra money. The motel was not in bad shape when we got it, so we had it up and running pretty quick. In the last four months we have had 8 guests complain of ghosts in room 15. One woman saw a body in the bathtub, but when we came to inspect it there was nothing. There were three incidents of someone beating on the door, but no one was there when they checked. They also heard screaming. The other reports were of screaming and the bathtub coming on by itself. We don't know what to do."

Your research will want to start with the history of the hotel. Was there a murder in room 15? Look for old newspaper articles. Once you find out what happened in room 15, research the people involved in the case. Was the suspect found? Who was the victim? Are there any relatives or witnesses to the case still around in your area?

Example 4:

"We have been living in our current house for the last 10 years, but just recently have had objects move around on their own. My

THE PROFESSIONAL GHOST INVESTIGATOR

husband said that when he came home a chair was in midair. He turned on a lamp to get a better look and the chair fell to the floor. We don't know why this is happening but we want it to stop."

In this case the location may not be the first thing you want to research since the married couple has been established in their house for 10 years. You should ask about the time things started to happen and if the couple bought or received any new items at that point. Perhaps a relative sent them a trinket from Mexico. Perhaps the couple collects some kind of antique item. Since this has the potential to also be a poltergeist you will want to check the stress levels of the married couple.

Example 5:

"I think my daughter is possessed. She's been acting strange for the last month. Can you help?"

A claim of possession is pretty serious whether it's true or false. You will want to start out by asking about religious affiliations and why the family has not contacted a religious authority. This should be followed up by getting a history of the girl and the family. Ask what the possessed girl was doing just before the possession is thought to have started. Ask if the client has any video, photographs, or audio recordings that you can review. Perform some research on the client's religious affiliations to see how their beliefs deal with possession, but don't notify the religious officials yet. Your preliminary investigation may be shorter than other cases. You need to prepare for collecting evidence of possession.

Once you've collected enough documentation, which might take a few days to two weeks, you can give the group a full report on what to expect before the actual investigation. It may sound a little longwinded, but it's really not hard to remember. In a nutshell:

1. Interview the client using a voice recorder.

2. Take statement using a voice recorder.
3. Try to get some sort of visual or do a walkthrough.
4. Research.

See Appendix II for Investigation Forms.

Clients & Cases

Clients come in all shapes and sizes. You need to be prepared to deal with people that come your way. You will generally find that clients fit into three categories: Believers, Skeptics, and Non-Believers. For your convenience the following are generalizations about these three groups. It helps to figure out your client so you can adjust your approach with them.

Believers will have their own views on what is going on, but they will usually accept almost everything you have to say. Sometimes the believers will get in your way simply because they are curious. They can be overly emotional if you find a believer who is not very objective.

Skeptics want to believe, but they just can't allow themselves that luxury without proof. Often times these people are more objective then believers or non-believers. They often won't get in your way, but occasionally you get a real jerk who wants to know everything that you and your group do.

Non-Believers simply don't believe whatsoever. They may claim an "act of God" or "simply nature", but they usually do not budge on their beliefs. You will find a lot of military, very religious, and public-oriented career people, like politicians or police commissioners, in this category.

Client Tactics

- **Courtesy** – Show your client courtesy. Be respectful to them, their beliefs, and their environment. You either have a client that has come to you or you are investigating an old case/legend and are trying to talk to a witness. Do not get angry with a client. Be as cordial and neutral as you can, if you feel anger or annoyance coming on.

- **Professionalism** – You need to approach your client in a professional manner. You need to be dressed appropriately, have your equipment ready for your preliminary investigation, have your forms ready for the client, and follow the GHOST INVESTIGATION etiquette.

- **Limited Contact** – There is no need for your entire group to be present while meeting the client the first time. One or two team members are plenty. You don't want to scare off your client simply by being over-eager for a case. Evaluate the case and the client before arranging for them to meet your team, something that should happen during the actual investigation.

- **Confidentiality** – Your client's privacy is important. You need to have a privacy arrangement form ready for them to sign, to guarantee their privacy. Ask before using equipment to record anything during your preliminary investigation. Your client needs to feel safe with you taking their case.

- **Information Sharing** – Your client will want to know what they will get out of this whole ordeal. You will also want to share with your client your possible use of their data. Have an Information Sharing Form ready to fill out. Be ready to respect their unwillingness to share their information or to keep their names a secret.

These tactics will guarantee that at least 80% of your clients will respond well to you and your team. Take into consideration that personality conflicts, high stress, rude behavior, and disbelief may play a strong part in that 20% that don't respond well.

Using Film to Understand Client Tactics

Watch *Poltergeist*, *The Frighteners*, *Rose Red*, and any episode of *Scooby Doo*.

- How did the investigators deal with their clients?
- What were the professional qualities?
- What were the amateur qualities?
- How did the lead investigator(s) share information with their teammates?

Religion & Spirituality of Your Client

In Chapter 1, you learned to leave your religious views at home. I am now telling you that you are going to have be accepting of other people's religions and spiritual views. Remember, you are approaching this as objectively as you possibly can, so you cannot have a religious bias. Consider yourself simply "well informed" on your own religion, just as a folklorist might be "well informed" on *Grimm's Fairy Tales*.

Chances are your client is religious in some sense, as most of the world is. You will want to know your client's religious beliefs if you suspect malicious spirits, possession, poltergeists, or if they simply want a house blessing. Every religion has methods of dealing with spirits, blessings, and other spiritual issues. Your attempt to do this according to your client's belief system is a 100% sign of courtesy and professionalism.

There are times when using your client's belief system isn't the best idea. These are minimal cases usually dealing with strong intellectual spirits or daimons. This could be anything from malicious spirits from an old tribal burial ground to negative spiritual activity from an old relic. If this is the case, you should first try to pinpoint the origin of the spirits, and then use methods from that culture and/or time period to remove the spirit(s).

The methods that you choose to use during your investigation process need to be run by your client first. They might want to know why their house smells like burnt sage or why you have a circle of white candles burning on their new hardwood floors, etc.

Potential Cases

Finding potential cases on your own is not always as easy as it sounds. You can investigate local legends and rumors, but after a while you will want to start looking into *live cases*, cases that are currently active. One way to start is by going online and pursuing social media venues like Facebook, Twitter, and starting a blog.

Another way to find live cases would be to post a small ad in your local newspaper. I recommend posting it in the Saturday and Sunday editions since those are typically the most circulated editions. Newspaper ads can work well, especially if you have an email or web address for people to check out in their spare time.

Network around your area to get yourself known. Start by posting flyers at local occult shops, herb/natural/health food stores, and coffee shops. It's best to talk to the shop owners or workers to let them know what you do and that you are currently looking for cases.

In some areas there are fairs or conventions for the paranormal or psychics. Do some research and find out if there is something in or near your area. This is a great place to network whether you set up an informational booth or to just spend some time at.

However you plan on finding new potential cases, be aware that everyone you talk to will have a story to tell you. It might be something that they saw, it might be something a family member saw, or it might be something that someone else saw. They could be total non-believers, but they will still have some sort of story. You will have to weed out the fluff and go after the good stuff. You need to look for current cases where your help is required.

Seeking Out Special Cases

Looking for *special cases*, those cases that are well known, possessions, or extremely active spirits, are hard to come by. You need to have some experience under your belt before you really go after the special cases.

If you are avidly out to find a special case to investigate, I recommend starting out with a well-known case. A well-known case would be something that you may read about in books or find scattered online or even know about just be living in your area. Perhaps it's a road haunted by black dogs or a white lady in some old mansion-turned-hotel or even a location where if you do a certain ritual, like walking around a tree backwards thirteen times, something will happen. These are the most common types of special cases and they are the easiest to start out with.

Be sure to get the proper permissions from people when you do special cases. If what you are looking for is on public land, like a road or a park, you are probably okay to not seek permission unless you have the potential to block someone's driveway or if the park is shut down at night. If you are at a cemetery, you will want to talk to public works, if the cemetery gets locked up at night.

Chapter 5 Quiz

Define

Baseline Information

Believers

Non-Believers

Skeptics

Questions

1. What are the basic W's?
2. What is an activity log?
3. What should be included in an activity log?
4. Who should keep an activity log?
5. Why is baseline information important?
6. List three things that you might include in baseline information.
7. What is initial research?
8. What should you bring to an interview?
9. Give a name and description for your basic three types of clients.
10. Name five ways to look for potential cases.
11. If you are Catholic, how do you approach your client's case?
12. What is a *special case*?
13. Name the five basic client tactics and provide a description.
14. If you were going to investigate a well-known local case about a grey lady who was known to wander down part of Main Street and enter an old hotel where she would promptly vanish in the lobby, who would you seek permission to investigate from? Why?
15. When should you not use your client's belief system as the basis for dealing with spirits?

Chapter 6 – The Investigation

The investigation is the most popular and exploited area of ghost investigation. This is the part where investigators go to a site and actively collect information with their equipment. It's not just a matter of showing up with an EMF detector and a voice recorder though. There are safety precautions, set-up basics, investigation etiquette, and other things that everyone needs to know before taking the plunge into the hands-on portion of the investigation process. The best piece of advice I can give you is to be well prepared because every case is different, but none will ever totally go 100% as planned.

Investigation Safety

Before any investigation occurs, the safety procedures should be run through. It may be as simple as letting everyone know that they have a first aid kit and to pay attention while wandering around in a dark building or it could be something more drastic like going over broken bone safety procedures.

Don't write off any safety procedures, no matter how whimsical they may seem to you, just understand that paranormal investigators go to outside location, cemeteries, old buildings, lakes/rivers, etc. These are all places where you could sprain an ankle, get a nasty cut, have a possible animal/insect attack, have an allergic reaction, or any number of other things.

The first thing that you should absolutely address is dressing for the location. Bring up weather reports and information on the location. Will the temperature be dropping during the night? Does the location you will be at have heat? Is it well insulated? What about rain? Is the area rocky or flat? Are there rusted pieces of equipment lying around? Is there water nearby that produces fog? Dressing properly will allow you and your team the peace of mind about their clothing choices. No one wants to worry about being cold, being wet, wearing sneakers instead of rain boots, or wearing shorts instead of long pants through the woods.

You will also want someone who is on first aid duty. While it's a good idea for your whole group to be certified in first aid and CPR, that might not happen for a few cases depending on when the local Red Cross is offering first aid and CPR classes. You must have at least one person who can handle basic first aid. They will be in charge of making sure that there is a first aid kit, perhaps a few emergency blankets, and anything else they think is essential. The person on first aid duty needs to be able to think clearly in a stressful situation in case something like a broken bone or a sprain or a deep gouge does occur. Make sure that everyone is aware of who is on first aid duty.

Give each person in the group a blank map of the area that you will be going to. It can be hand-drawn, computer-drawn, or a copy of schematics. Everyone needs to be aware of the area. Have everyone on the case mark up the *hot spots*, the areas with the most or constant ghost activity, themselves. At this time divide people into teams of two or three and station them in sections. It is also a good idea to divide up the areas of the map if you choose to work in a grid formation or by floors, etc. This will reduce any confusion when you get to the site. It will also allow everyone to know where everyone else should be.

Main Floor Level

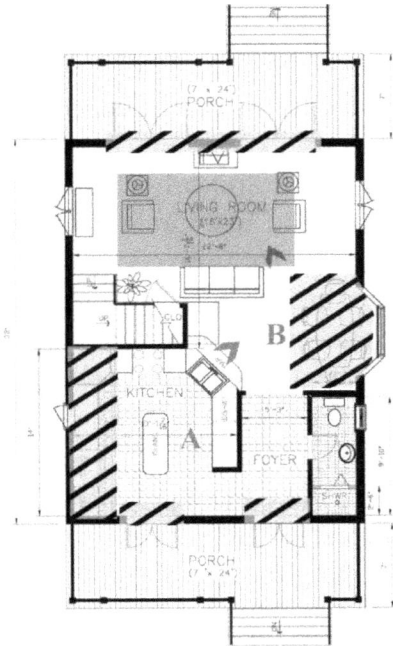

2nd Floor Level

Camera - The point is the camera with the two arms indicating the view of the camera.

Stripes indicates areas of major occurences with ghost.

Grey indicates where Home Base is.

A   Letters indicate where teams are.

When you design a set up plan, you will want the groups to be in each major area. Use a highlighter on a blank map to indicate where activity has taken place. This should help in figuring out how many people need to be on-site. Is it a two team job? Do you need three teams? How many stationary cameras do you need to have available? Where should they be facing? Be sure to either indicate or talk about the range of each team. In the image above, teams A and B have relatively little room to move in, but team C has the entire second floor to themselves. Teams A and B could also be made up of 3 people collectively, that is one person stays in section A, one in section B, and one transient teammate between the two, most likely the person trying to get an EVP in order to reduce noise pollution.

While you are planning out the locations on the map, give people a time for a mid-investigation break. People can eat food, drink some water, check their email, and other stuff during this time. It helps relieve stress and tension among the group. If any groups are going to change locations, you can plan it around mid-investigation breaks. It's best to keep the breaks limited to 10-30 minutes. Make sure everyone brings something to drink and something to eat, preferably healthy items as they will keep you more alert than junk food.

The last thing that you may want to remind your team about is spiritual protection. This will vary from person to person, but through nearly all cultures, salt is a constant purifier and protector. As a general rule, it's best to have a box of salt on hand for emergency purposes. Allow your team to pick and choose their personal protective items. While we are trying to remain objective about the case, we all have different ways of protecting our selves. When it comes to self-protection, go with what you are comfortable using whether it's a cross, a Star of David, or a lucky rabbit's foot.

Equipment Test

As soon as your team is through the safety measures for the case, you will need to have an equipment check. Make sure that everyone has a flashlight, notebook, and pen or pencil. If you are using walkie-talkies then make sure each team has one that works. Be sure to check everything for batteries and make sure you have extra on hand. This goes for camera and video camera batteries too. Use the Equipment Checklist on the next page to help you organize your team better.

Your first aid kit needs to be kept up to date. If your team seems to go through Band-Aids like candy, then make sure that you always have an extra box on hand. If you have a team member that is always asking for a Kleenex, then you may want to start keeping that with the first aid kit. Your first aid kit should be fairly compact in itself, but with the addition of blankets and extra supplies, you might want to dedicate a duffle bag simply to first aid. Some additional items that you might want in your first aid kit are:

• Blankets • Extra Band-Aids • Extra Ace Bandages • Smelling Salt • Ice Pack • Hand Sanitizer • Bottle of Water • Rubbing Alcohol	• List of Team Member Allergies • Nitrile Gloves • Splint • Various creams and ointments like Calamine Lotion, Anti-Itch Cream, etc • Tums or Rolaids • Towel or Rags • Nail Clippers & File • Safety Glasses

Be sure that any extra supplies are also checked. This might include any new equipment that is being tested, appropriate gloves for the location, and equipment for the home base. Home base equipment may include lamps, tables, computers, chairs, etc.

Equipment Checklist		Case	
First Aid Duty	Basic First Aid	Additional	Additional
	☐ Full Kit ☐ Extra Band-aids ☐ Extra Ace Bandage	☐ Blanket Amount_____	
Home Base Manager			
	☐ Base Set Up Plan ☐ Base Equipment	☐ Water for Team ☐ Food for Team	
Team Member	Flashlight	Equipment	Equipment
	☐ Working ☐ Extra batteries	Type: ☐ Working ☐ Extra batteries	Type: ☐ Working ☐ Extra batteries
	☐ Working ☐ Extra batteries	Type: ☐ Working ☐ Extra batteries	Type: ☐ Working ☐ Extra batteries

	☐ Working ☐ Extra batteries	Type: ☐ Working ☐ Extra batteries	Type: ☐ Working ☐ Extra batteries
	☐ Working ☐ Extra batteries	Type: ☐ Working ☐ Extra batteries	Type: ☐ Working ☐ Extra batteries
	☐ Working ☐ Extra batteries	Type: ☐ Working ☐ Extra batteries	Type: ☐ Working ☐ Extra batteries

Home Base

Home base is where your group starts and stops. It's the control center and the meeting place. Some groups use a small motor home while others set up a screen house (a tent-like shelter) with a rainfly or an indoor set up of portable tables, chairs, etc. The home base should be centrally located at the site. Your first aid kit, extra supplies, and any food/drink items for investigation breaks should remain at the home base. This is also where your client can remain for the duration of the investigation, unless invited to a particular area by the investigators.

Home base should be run by a home base manager. This person is essentially like dispatch. They are in charge of walkie-talkies, maintaining the home base, keeping the first aid kit accessible, and possibly monitoring a surveillance set-up. If there is any need for 911, the home base manager should be the one to call it in. Phone calls for the group should be routed to the home base manager for the purpose of managing possible disruptions during the investigation.

Investigation Etiquette

Investigation etiquette is made up of common sense and awareness of those around you. Due to the basic nature of the etiquette, it can be overlooked, so it needs to be stated for everyone's benefit.

- **Silence** – During an investigation there is a *strict code of silence* unless you have a voice recorder in your hand or you are setting up a video camera. When setting up a video camera, you need to state the date, time, location, and who is in the team(s) that might be seen on the camera. If you have a voice recorder, you are going to spend your time during the investigation asking questions in an attempt to get an EVP. You will also need to make note of any noises that your voice recorder may pick up such as "Steve just dropped his flashlight" or "Linda's foot hit a pipe that was on the floor", so that way the noises do not become mistaken for paranormal sounds.

- **No Smells** – No one should be wearing perfume or cologne, smell of cigarette smoke, or have any other smell to their person. This could interfere with ghostly smells experienced by team members.

- **Silent Phones** – No one should be using their cell phones during an investigation, but if people insist on having them then insist that they are on silent and left at home base. People can make phone calls or text during the investigation break. Some people will use their phone in place of a watch though which is the main exception for phones during investigations, but does it cost that much for a watch?

- **Follow the Team Leader** – Whoever is in charge of the investigation, the Lead Investigator, you need to follow their instructions. During the investigation, the Home Base Manager will be second in command. You might have an idea, which you should share, but don't take it personally if the Lead or the Manager don't go for it. It's business, not personal.

Investigation Procedure Guidelines

Investigations are fairly simple in nature. Essentially, you go to your chosen location, you get your home base set up, the teams get set up, and everyone splits up to investigate and previously planned. Investigations don't always go as planned and sometimes it is best to start with a set of guidelines.

Step 1	When you get to your location everyone needs to help set up the home base area. This will include placing any stationary cameras, hooking up the walkie-talkies and other pieces of equipment, setting up or preparing a shelter if needed, and just making sure that everything is in order.
Step 2	This step sounds childish, but make sure that people hit the toilets, turn off their phones, and are prepared for the investigation.
Step 3	Each team should be ready to investigate. In each team, everyone should have a flashlight and up to two pieces of equipment. Be sure to have extra batteries with you. The problem with a team trying to handle all types of equipment is that voice recording equipment will pick up the shuffling between equipment and that might be read as false "ghostly" noises. A good team combination is: Person A – EMF and voice recorder, and Person B – Digital camera. No two people working together should have the same equipment unless you are after a certain type of results.
Step 4	When you head out with your teammate to investigate remember to maintain the strict policy of silence. The exceptions being a sighting, warning of a dangerous or potentially dangerous area, something happening to your person, or

	making/receiving a call via walkie-talkie.
Step 5	Upon reaching your investigation area, be sure to let your Home Base Manager know, unless you are in visual range of him/her. Have a map of the area and your notepad ready. Record the time when you and your partner officially start in your area. Use your equipment and keep an ongoing activity log. If you found anything that you feel needs immediate attention, you should radio to home base so the team can reorganize.
Step 6	At the time of the investigation break, the Home Base Manager will call the teams in. Finish what you are doing and head back to base.

These are the general guidelines for an investigation, though you will find that steps 3-6 will be repeated until the end of the investigation. When the investigation wraps up, put your things away and help break down the home base area. This might mean gathering any trash, putting equipment away, taking down any shelter that was set up, etc.

Investigation Problems

You will find that during your investigation you may come across some common problems. The following is a list of problems with recommended solutions.

- **Weather Changes** – The weather can change at the drop of a hat. It's best to wear layers, which might be your solution, and it's also a good idea to have limits. If you have an outdoor location you are investigating and its pouring down rain, wait until the next day or until the weather clears up.

- **Accidents** – Accidents can occur in just about any situation, more so when you are working in poorly lit or dark areas. Make sure everyone on the team is alert, give people ample time during investigation breaks to have some coffee or food, and make sure you have a designated person on First Aid Duty. If something happens while people are broken up into teams, have them report to the Home Base Manager.

- **Hoax** – If the reported area is an obvious hoax have the Home Base Manager call everyone back and simply leave. A *hoax* is a situation that gets reported as true even though the person reporting it knows that it not true and is usually done as a trick or joke.

- **Too Many People** – At times you will have an extra team member show up who is not scheduled to be on a case or a member will bring a girlfriend/boyfriend/friend/sibling along. The extra person has to leave. Your cases are not public forums. You are trying to run an investigation where you are collecting data. This might mean that you have a team member who has to leave with their extra person, so be ready to deal with that. You do not need every team member on every case and you definitely don't need inexperienced non-team members on the scene.

- **The Fussy Team Member** – Eventually you will get a fussy team member. They are usually the person who grumbles over everything, are often negative, don't follow directions, and starts problems with other team members. You will have to dismiss them from your group entirely. They will bring down the others and will create enough problems to make people leave the group. Discretely pull the fussy team member aside and tell them that they need to shape up or ship out. If you have to tell them again, dismiss them.

- **Drama Queen** – Many people who want to be a ghost investigator have seen the TV shows and believe that you have to possess a certain amount of drama on every case. These drama queens will frequently break the silence policy during investigations to report every noise they hear. They will freak out over common objects/noises and their feelings. This is something you do not want to deal with. They will ruin your investigation by creating noise pollution and contaminating other evidence. This is another case where you need to discretely tell them to shape up or ship out. Since these people need to be the center of attention, you may want to try having them as Home Base Manager.

- **The Smelly Teammate** – There always seems to be the one person who smokes or who douses themselves in perfume/cologne. If you have someone show up to an investigation who can't help but smoke while investigating or who just can't stay away from the perfume/cologne, you need to tell them to leave. They can compromise an investigation by distorting the evidence.

- **Always Late** – If you have a team member who is always late, you need to talk to them. Five minutes late is one thing, but if they are constantly late at random times (like 5-30 minutes late) then you need to address it. Your group is not important enough, they are too busy, or their interest has waned. There is no excuse for constant lateness when you pre-schedule meetings and investigations.

- **Unruly Clients** – Every once in a while you will get an unruly client. They might be drunk, using drugs, being obnoxious, getting in the way, or taking on the role of drama queen. If they are drunk or using drugs, do not investigate at that time. If they are being obnoxious, getting in the way, or are taking on the role of drama queen, station them with the Home Base Manager unless you absolutely need them.

- **The Entity Becomes Violent** – If the entity goes from mild to violent, you need to be ready to take some immediate action. If you are inside, salt the doors and windows. If you are outside, create a circle of salt. This is just for basic protection. You should report to home base and be ready to perform a basic blessing. If a basic blessing only calms it down, you will have to delve deeper into the realm of expelling ghosts.

Basic Blessings

The following are a variety of house blessing and area clearing methods used by various religions. A house blessing or clearing is essentially a clearing of negative energy or spirits from a specific area. In chapter 3 you were given a shamanistic method of ritual clearing and a wiccan method for a "New Home Major Cleansing Spell". They are fairly basic, non-offensive, and easy to perform. The following is a specific list of religion-based methods of clearing. These should be done if there is an immediate disturbance and/or if the client specifically asks for something to be done.

Christian House Blessings

The Christian faith has a variety of prayers, depending on what branch of Christianity a person belongs to, but the actions are the same. A person of religious authority moves from room to room saying a prayer while sprinkling holy water or oil. Olive oil can be used for this purpose.

Catholic

Repeat this prayer in every room while holding a cross and sprinkling holy water or oil.

"O heavenly Father, Almighty God, we humbly beseech Thee to bless and sanctify this house and all who dwell therein and everything else in it, and do Thou vouch to fill it with all good things; grant to them, O Lord, the abundance of heavenly blessings and from the richness of the earth every substance necessary for life, and finally direct their desires to the fruits of Thy mercy. At our entrance, therefore, deign to bless and sanctify this house as Thou didst deign to bless the house of Abraham, of Isaac, and of Jacob; and may the angels of Thy light, dwelling within the walk of this house, protect it and those who dwell therein. Through Christ our Lord. Amen."

Protestant

This is what the Protestant's call "Chalking the Door". You will need chalk. It finishes with everyone speaking together.

Person of religious authority: "Lord Jesus, through your Incarnation and birth in true human form, you have made all the earth holy. We now ask your blessing upon this simple gift of your creation — chalk. We use it as a tool to teach our children, and they use it as a tool in their play and games. Now, with your blessing, may it become a tool for us to mark the doors of our home with the symbols of your wise servants who, so long ago, came to worship and adore you in your first home."

People in turn mark the doorway with one or more of the symbols:

"C M B" and/or the year (like "2012")

Person of religious authority: "May we, in this house, and all who come to visit, to work, and to play, remember these things throughout the coming year. May all who come and go here find peace, comfort, joy, hope, love, and salvation, for Christ has come to dwell in this house and in these hearts."

All: "May we be Christ's light in the world. Amen."

Anglican

The Anglican's have a long process with suggested prayers for each type of room. They say a prayer in each room while a cross is present and holy water or oil is sprinkled.

The main entrance of the house.

"Father in heaven, I stand in faith and on the authority I have as a believer in Jesus Christ. In the name of Jesus Christ, I bind every evil spirit and every evil plan made for this home. I cancel the enemy's plans and call forth God's plans for this home. In the name of Jesus Christ, by the power of His cross and blood, I bind any spirits, powers and forces and command that you may not speak, manifest, or move about this home. You may do nothing. You have no power here. God's word says that God has plans for good and not evil for us (Jeremiah 29:11) and I claim those plans now. I rebuke any curses, hexes, or spells sent against us or this property and send them directly to Jesus for Him to deal with as He will. Lord, I cover myself and everyone around me with the blood of Jesus. I cover (call them by name) with the blood of Jesus. I cover this home with the blood of Jesus. In the Name of Jesus Christ, by the power of His blood, I break off every power of the kingdom of darkness and cancel every argument that has established itself against the plans of God for this home and for each of us, and spoil every attack of the enemy. I call forth, in the name of Jesus, all of God's plans and purposes for this day and for our lives. Satan, the blood of Jesus is against you and you have no authority in this place or over any of us. Father, as we undertake this work to which you have called us, I ask that your will be done. I give thanks to you and I praise to you. **Amen.**

"Peace be with this house and with all who live here. Blessed be the name of the Lord."

Followed by Revelations 3:20 and Psalm 121:1-8.

Bedrooms.

Recite Isaiah 32:17-18) and Psalm 3:1-9.

Child's bedroom.

Recite Matthew 19:14 and Psalm 127:1-6.

Living room.

Recite 1 Peter 4:8-11 and Psalm 16:1-11.

Kitchen.

Recite John 6:27, 33-35 and Psalm 23:1-6.

Dining Room.

Recite Luke 22:26b-27 and Psalm 146:1-9.

Main Bathroom.

Recite Proverbs 11:24-25 and Psalm 1:1-6.

Office or Study.

Recite Deuteronomy 6:4-7 and Psalm 25:3-14.

Work Room.

Recite Colossians 3:23-24 and Psalm 34:9-14.

Garage and Storage.

Recite Matthew 6:19-21 and Psalm 33:1-11.

Orthodox

It is customary, to invite your priest to bless your home with holy water within a few weeks following Theophany. Prepare by cleaning the house and opening and lighting all the rooms. The items needed for a house blessing are:

- Icon of Christ
- candle
- large serving bowl for the Holy Water
- incense
- incense burner

- Charcoal
- A sprig of basil leaves (available at the grocery store.)

Many of these items can be purchased in the church bookstore. Place the items on a small table. The priest blesses the water by dipping a cross in it and repeating a blessing. Using the basil sprig dipped in water as a sprinkler, he will go to each room and sprinkle it in the four corners blessing the home with the grace of the Holy Spirit which also protects you from evil spirits. Save some of the holy water in a bottle in your ikonostasi (home altar) and pour the remainder on plants. Although ideal, all family members do not need to be present for the house blessing. House Blessings are a yearly tradition.

Personal Use of Holy Water

According to Orthodox doctrine, holy water has the power to sanctify and heal. Have each family member drink a small amount of the holy water from Epiphany or the home blessing. Keep the unused holy water in your home ikonostasi for future use: times of adversity, before starting a new venture or trip, to give thanks, or when someone is ill. You may drink it or anoint yourself when you feel spiritually afflicted. To rid the house of evil spirits, it should be sprinkled in the four corners of each room, so no one will step on it. In rural Greece the holy water is sprinkled in the fields and on the animals.

Jewish

In Jewish households, the following passages are actually written on a small piece of paper that is placed in a case (called a mezuzah) which is attached to all the exterior doors. Use Deuteronomy 6:4-9 and 11:13-21. These should be placed on the doors and gates of the home.

The Hindu Puja

The Hindu ritual for blessing a house is called Puja. It is comprised of 16 steps (shodasha upachara) that are common in all varieties of puja and is performed in front of the family's chosen deity such as Ganesha or Kali:

1. *Avahana* ("invocation"). The deity is invited to the ceremony from the heart.
2. *Asana*. The deity is offered a seat.
3. *Padya*. The deity's feet are symbolically washed.
4. Water is offered for washing the head and body
5. *Arghya*. Water is offered so the deity may wash its mouth.
6. *Snana* or *abhisekha*. Water is offered for symbolic bathing.
7. *Vastra* ("clothing"). Here a cloth may be wrapped around the image and ornaments affixed to it.
8. *Upaveeda* or *Mangalsutra*. Putting on the sacred thread.
9. *Anulepana* or *gandha*. Perfumes and ointments are applied to the image. Sandalwood paste or kumkum is applied.
10. *Pushpa*. Flowers are offered before the image, or garlands draped around its neck.
11. *Dhupa*. Incense is burned before the image.
12. *Dipa* or *Aarti*. A burning lamp is waved in front of the image.
13. *Naivedya*. Foods such as cooked rice, fruit, clarified butter, sugar, and betel leaf are offered.
14. *Namaskara* or *pranama*. The worshipper and family bow or prostrate themselves before the image to offer homage.
15. *Parikrama* or *Pradakshina*. Circumbulation around the deity.

16. Taking leave.

Buddhist House Blessing

A Buddhist house blessing involves making an offering, chanting, and sprinkling holy water. Traditionally the offering is a meal of red fish, rice with adzuki beans, and a small bottle of saki. Other items can be offered. All offering should be placed before a representation of Buddha. In each room of the house holy water must be sprinkled as you chant the following:

"May the clouds of the Blessed One's spiritual powers,
His unrivalled knowledge and boundless compassion,
Pour down upon your house like a monsoon rain,
Nurturing the roots of your wholesome qualities.

"May the Dhamma as doctrine, path, and fruition,
As Nibbana the Deathless, the state beyond sorrow,
Infuse your home with the glory of truth
And make it an oasis for thirsty seekers.

"May the wavelike blessings of the Sangha-jewel,
From Sariputta and Moggala to the present-day Order,
Dispel all threats from the forces of darkness
And envelop your home with the aura of purity.

"May the three discourses of protective might–
The Metta, Ratana, and Mangala Suttas–
Resound like a chorus of celestial angels,
Bringing you success in all you undertake.

"May the Dhamma-protectors in all ten directions,
The gods in the heavens and the nagas of the earth,
Ward off all dangers, misfortunes, and hazards,
And ensure you live happily in your new abode.

May you dwell at home like monks in the forest,
Delighting in meditation, devoted to good works.
May your home shine brightly like a heavenly palace,
A beacon of Dhamma giving solace to all beings."

Wiccan House Blessing

This is a blessing where burning is involved, so take precaution. Grind dragon's blood and frankincense together in a mortar with a pestle. In each room of the house, burn the blended powder over charcoal. Allow the smoke to fill each room. You can make a verbal blessing at this time, if you wish, but it is not required.

Wiccan Floorwash

Boil 3 cups of water and a few sprigs of basil, hyssop, and pine needles. Let this boil down to a cup of water, creating an herbal infusion. Add this to a bucket of water. Add in a cup of vinegar. Wash all floors of the house. If you have carpeting, wash the walls.

Mayan House Cleansing

Place yourself in a meditative state and try to communicate with the Earth Lord. Make peace with all of the various beings in the house, starting with the Earth Lord working up to the beings in the home. Traditionally, Mayan houses are built with earthen floors, so a hole is dug in the floor's center to open up communication with the Earth Lord. You may have to perform this ritual in the basement, literally under the house, or under an awning.

An altar is built on the floor, usually where the negativity is most concentrated, behind a protective row of pine branches, candles, food, and drink in an attempt to appease the spirits. Copal and herbs are smudged, and blessed water is sprinkled around the house to soak up any residual negative energy and to reinstate a positive dimension. The family should prepare a special meal in which friends and family are welcome to dine as a celebration of peace and well-being in the home.

Create an Emergency Blessing Kit

In case you need to perform a house blessing and you were not prepared for it before hand, it would be wise to have an emergency blessing kit ready at your fingertips. Using the basic blessings listed, create a list of items that you might need for an emergency blessing kit. List the texts that you need copies of for your kit. Do you have all of the supplies? Are there any supplies that you are going to have trouble finding?

Chapter 6 Quiz

Define

Home Base

Questions

1. Name four investigation safety measures.
2. What are the points of investigation etiquette?
3. What is the *strict code of silence* and what are the exceptions?
4. What are the basic steps for an investigation?
5. What sort of problems can take place during an investigation?
6. What is a house blessing and when should it be performed?
7. What are the constants for nearly all Christian-based house blessings?

Chapter 7 – Post-Investigation

Post-Investigation

The post-investigation is a collecting and sharing of investigation information and a presentation for the client. This is important because it gives each case closure and the client gets a nice pretty package. Essentially the post-investigation gives the group a chance to go through their collected readings/ photos/video/audio/etc, so the client doesn't have to.

If any scientific analysis needs to be done, say for example that the investigator collect some ectoplasm, physical matter excreted by mediums and psychics due to spirit activity. The ectoplasm, and the results of the ectoplasm analysis, would be post-investigation work. Never do any scientific analysis yourself because it will be viewed by the scientific community as biased. You need to have a third party analyze any hard evidence.

Before any analysis of hard evidence is done, give your group a deadline. This might be a week or perhaps a presentation at the next meeting.

Analyzing Hard Evidence
Visual Evidence

It takes time to go through what you collected during your investigation. Using the Double Take Method is very efficient. The double take method is a way to reduce your work load and it works well with any visual mediums. Start by skimming through your files. Every time you think you might have something, mark down the photo name or video time, and continue with your first take of your evidence. When you finish with your first take, go back for your second take. This time around you will want to focus on what you marked down.

After using the double take method, you can go back through your evidence at your own pace with your focus being between your marked files/times. There might have been something that you missed, perhaps some audio on film or a light orb on a light background.

Once you have your photos or video examined look at what you have. Try to explain what it is. Is it a reflection? Could it be dust or insects? Was someone smoking?

Audio Evidence

Audio evidence is pretty straight forward. Listen to your recording all the way through. Be sure that you are actively listening to it. I recommend doing something simple to keep your hands busy while you listen, like crossword puzzles, Sudoku, knitting, cleaning house, etc. Make sure that you crank the volume up. Some voices will not be heard at standard levels. Mark down the time of any potential evidence.

Once you go through the first time, you can go back and listen to the points of interest that you marked down. Try to determine what is causing the sounds. Was it a sound from a different room or area? Was it your teammate? Was it something being moved?

EMF, Temperature, and Other Evidence

Graph all EMF, Temperature, and other readings from equipment. On a graph, X should indicate Time and Y should indicate Levels. The two graphs below are examples of an

EMF graph and a Temperature graph. This is a great way to show your findings in a visual and informational way.

Sensory evidence should be written up in your report, but could also be graphed if there are repeated incidents. Sensory evidence is comprised of smells, tastes, and feelings, but nothing visual or tangibly physical.

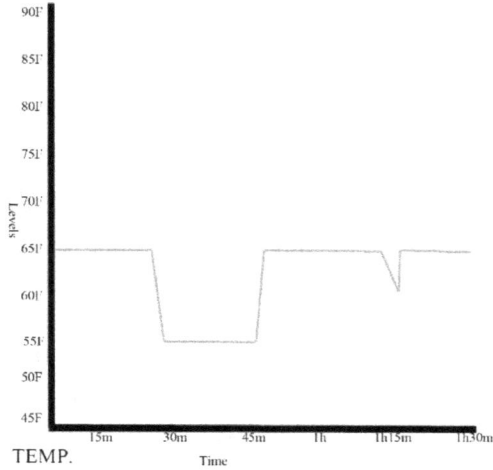

Other evidence that you may come across is tangible physical evidence, or evidence that you can physically touch. This could be ectoplasm, items inexplicably deposited in a certain area, bones, physical attacks, and anything else that you can touch or pick up. Take video footage and pictures. This evidence should be documented to the best of your ability. If there is blood, take a clean sample. If someone is physically attacked by a violent spirit, take photos and immediately go to a hospital for an examination by a doctor. Evidence should be collected and contained.

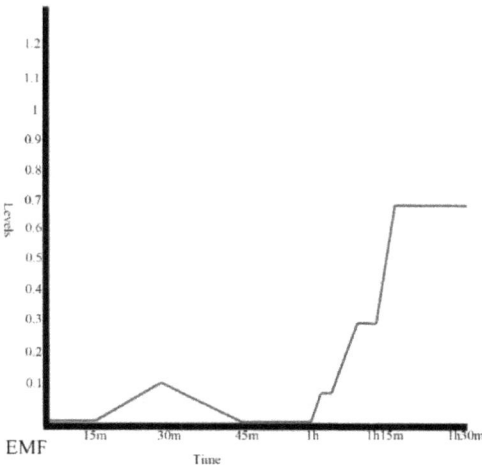

Collecting Samples & Evidence

If you have an incident where you need to collect samples and evidence then you should follow these steps. You will need nitrile gloves, collection bags/vials, and other equipment. Its best to approach evidence and sample collecting as a lab technician or a crime scene investigator would.

1. Take measurements and photographs of the samples or evidence that you plan to collect. Use standard measurement items like a ruler, a standard coin, or tape measure. Do not use your hand, your shoe, a banana or anything else that has inconsistent size.
2. Figure out the best way to collect the sample based on the following two methods.

Blood and Other Liquid Samples

1. Put on nitrile gloves.
2. You will need a sterile vial with screw cap or a sterile jar with screw cap to hold samples, and a sterile cotton swab.
3. Open the vial or jar and the cotton swab from its packet. Take a sample with the swab and immediately place it in the vial or jar, including cotton swab. Screw the cap on the vial or jar.
4. Label the vial or jar.

Solid Evidence

1. Put on nitrile gloves.
2. You will want to place the solid evidence (bones, watches, books, etc) into paper bags, cardboard boxes, envelopes, or anti-static plastic bags. Plastic bags have the potential to create static electricity, which can ruin some evidence, and allows for the growth of mold and bacteria. Do not use Ziploc

> bags.
> 3. Label the bag/envelope/box.

Evidence needs to be bagged, tagged, and sealed. Try not to contaminate evidence. If you want to examine the evidence that you collected, you should do so in a very clean room. You can use a kitchen counter, but be sure to clean it with your normal cleaners and then again with a bleach-water solution of (1cup bleach, 2 cups water). The bleach-water solution will kill off any contaminates. It is best to examine collected evidence under good lighting and with magnifying glasses. These are both easily obtainable. Desk lamps or shop lamps with a clamp work well for lighting.

If you have blood or other liquid samples, do not examine them yourself. Find a laboratory in your area that can test the samples. In the phone book, look for: Chemists – Analytical, Laboratories (analytical, medical, research, testing), and Environmental Consultants. Call a laboratory to see if it's the proper laboratory for your needs. Take them a sample with photographs and a copy of your activity log during the time you collected the sample. The results you receive from the laboratory will be added to your final results.

Finding Haunted Objects

At times, you will come across objects that can create a haunted space. Often times these objects are new to their surroundings, despite their actual age. These objects can be anything, for example: shoes, dolls, a chair, a jewelry box, a painting, etc. Haunted objects are often collected while traveling, garage sales, estate sales, antique stores, heirlooms passed on to the next generation, items found left in a new purchase like a vehicle or a house, items found buried, and items stolen from the deceased. Its best to talk to an experienced collector of haunted items to learn how to deal with the item like John Zaffis (collecting for years) or the author of this book, Jessie Desmond (collecting for the last few years).

Coinciding Evidence

When your group gets back together to present what they have found through their collected evidence from the investigation, start looking for coinciding evidence. Coinciding evidence is evidence that occurred at the same time. For instance, if there is a team of two and one person has video evidence of an apparition moving through the room, perhaps the other person has audio evidence of the apparition at the same time.

Coinciding evidence is useful in determining the next steps of the investigation. You may find a new research venue through your evidence, you may find a definite hot spot, and you may find that you can now clear the area.

More Research

As a team, put together a new line of research for your case. You might have a name or a particular area to focus on now. You can think of this as research of depth, instead of your previous research of breadth. While you are looking at what to research, also think of who to talk to and where to go for research purposes.

Research will also involve contacting experts. It's important to stick with experts who have experience (a janitor of 20 years), graduate school degrees (a masters or a doctorate), or people with proper job titles (journeyman or executive or director). The people with these levels of expertise will make your research more viable.

Writing Reports

During the post-investigation, you will want to start writing your report. Be sure that your activity log is up to date and make sure that if you go over evidence that you write it down in your activity log. Many people hate writing reports, but it is very important for every case that you investigate, real or hoax. The best way to start writing a report is to pass out folders to every investigator. Their report, activity log, transcripts, evidence reports, photographs, maps, etc will go into their folder.

The activity log was discussed in Chapter 5, so please refer to that if you have questions. The Investigation Report can be started at any time. The format for the investigation report can be found on the next page.

Begin with the case name/number, the date or date range of the whole investigation, your current date, and your name. This should be in the upper left hand corner of the page. Use a standard font in size 12. Reports should be fairly uniform in style. This lends itself to professionalism.

The first few paragraphs should be an introduction to the case. If someone else is reading this case, they should know what has been going on, why the team was called in, if you have any theories, and what you were doing on the case.

Additional information will be needed before you start writing about your actual investigation. Take the time to write out information based on research. If you met with dead ends or false leads, include this information as well. If there is another problem in the future with this location, or even with a similar event, you will need to have as much information available to you as possible.

An investigation introduction is critical. This is where you should talk about who you were partnered up with, the equipment that you were using, the weather, the temperature, etc. Refer to the baseline information at this point.

The investigation should follow the introduction. This is strictly a blow by blow of activities that comes directly from your activity log.

List your equipment and what you found with that equipment. This should be a list of files or graphs. It can also be a summary of any samples or evidence collected with a reference to any laboratory reports.

Basic Report Format

Case name

Investigation date

Today's date

Your name

Introduction to the case. A general summary of what's been going on and what you're expecting.

Additional investigation information. What did you find out through your research? Were there any false leads or dead ends? Refer to photographs, interviews, or articles in your folder.

Investigation introduction. Tell us who you are partnered up with and what equipment you are using. If it's outdoor phenomenon, then please note the weather, temperature, and anything else that seems important. Was there a problem with any equipment? Did you try anything new?

The investigation. Using your activity log, give us a blow by blow of your investigation.

9:30 pm -Started investigation by taking photos of room 1, room 2, room 3, and the hall closet.

10:15pm – Finished taking photos. Used EMF detector in every room.

11:00 pm - Met back up with everyone at the main base (floor 1 kitchen).

Equipment.

Mentionable files or readings or time on film of occurrences, repeat this step for each piece of equipment

---

that you had results with.

Digital Camera:

DSC001.JPG

DSC002.JPG

DSC003.JPG

DSC004.JPG

DSC0014.JPG

DSC0015.JPG

DSC0017.JPG

EMF – See Graph.

Regroup information. This is where you can discuss your findings, coinciding findings, and the next plan of actions for the group.

Investigation 2. If you revisit the site for a second investigation, start again with the investigation introduction, the investigation, equipment, and regroup information.

Conclusion (aka your opinion for the end) What do you think was the cause of the results you had? Do you think the place needs to be revisited or some other option (exorcised, left alone, etc)? What sort of things would you do differently?

Document your team's findings, coinciding findings, and your team's plan of action. This is the closing paragraph for your first investigation. List any research plans or references that you wish to check into.

If you revisit the haunted location, which you may end up doing a number of times, go through and write up a whole new investigation section in your report. You can even label it *Investigation 1, Investigation 2,* and *Investigation 3.* Be sure to mention in your new investigation introduction what you researched based on your first investigation and how your methods for the new investigation have changed.

When you are finished, write a conclusion. This is your opinion of what was happening, what your research and investigations indicated, your final results, and what you recommend for the incident. If you have gone through a house blessing, then you may indicate that "nothing further needs to be done" or that you "should keep an eye on the location for future disturbing".

Chapter 7 Quiz

Define

Post-Investigation

Ectoplasm

Double Take Method

Coinciding Evidence

Questions

Who should analyze any findings?

How should you display EMF or Temperature findings?

What's the best way to analyze visual evidence?

What's the best way to analyze audio evidence?

What do you do if you find tangible physical evidence?

What are the key features of an investigation report?

Chapter 8 – Final Results

Your final results will be divided into two forms: Public and Client. Public results are tailored to the public to see. Client results are tailored for the client's eyes only. Public results are text and visual only, meaning that there will not be a disc of information available. Public results may also have the client's name altered from Mr. John Thomas to Mr. T, upon client request. Client results will be more in-depth.

The team leader will be responsible for putting together the final results into both a client package and a public package. The client package will be presented and given to the client, while the public package will be put together for public documentation.

It works best to present the client with a fastener folder that holds a copy of their case files and media files placed on disc. The public results are to be presented in a completely different manner. Public results should be presented annually or bi-annually in a printed journal format with no disc of media files, though pictures can be included through print. The public results can be printed locally or through an online self-publishing company, and a copy should be given to your local library as a local reference book.

Client Results

The client results are put together for the client. It consists of: a summary report, individual reports, scientific analysis reports, findings and other paperwork, and tailored media files. If the client asks for help clearing an area, this would be documented and added to the file for the client. The client may need or want a copy of the investigation to present to a real estate agent, as a family milestone, or to present to other interested parties (police, religious leader, etc) if there are further problems.

Reports

A copy of each investigator's report should be included in the file. This will give any reader a sense of where everybody was and what they were doing. It can also assist in further investigations if any problems arise after the ghost investigation is over.

The summary report should be put together by the lead investigator after all the individual reports are collected. It's basically a summary of what was found during the investigation and what was concluded in the post-investigation. Summary reports are typically one or two pages long.

Scientific Analysis Reports

Keep the original scientific analysis report and provide a copy of the report for the client. The scientific analysis provides court-worthy proof of what was found or not found. The client may be willing to pay for scientific analysis, but this will often fall to your ghost investigation team. Be sure that this analysis is done by a third party laboratory.

Tailored Media Files

Any media files, whether it is audio, video, or photos, needs to be trimmed down. If you take 200 photos and you have 10 photos of ghost activity, hand those 10 photos over to the client instead of all 200. If you have 4 hours of audio recording and you have a 2.5 second EVP, trim down an audio file so it is 5-10 seconds long.

All media that is going to be given over to the client should be put onto a standard CD. DO NOT have some reports digital and some printed out. Keep the reports to a printed format. Clients respond well to printed reports and media on CD.

Public Results

For public results the team will have to make everything digital in order to set up a book printing. Public results are a collection of investigations done by the ghost investigation team published annually or bi-annually. It is recommended that the team donates a copy of each printing to a local library. This provides a record of your investigations for public interest. You may find, after publishing a few collections of public results, that there are similar patterns, statistics, etc from your investigations. It's possible to gain more team members from the academic world if they can analyze your work.

The Client's Privacy

You need to check the privacy contract signed by your client. If they state that they do not want their full name or address listed for public interest, you need to stand by your contract. Change their names to Mr./Mrs./Miss *Client Initials*, like Mr.E.W.F or Miss J. When it comes to addresses, you can simply not include the house number.

Keep in mind that your client may remain in the house or build on a lot that is or was haunted. They could be worried about employers, neighbors, friends, or family finding out about their paranormal ordeal.

Everything Is Printed

When you are putting together your results, keep in mind that everything is going to be printed. While text is easy to print, you may have to adjust your pictures, maps, or other media files for the best printing quality. The best way to test your media is to print it out on a standard printer. If it looks good, then you don't have to mess with it, otherwise you will need someone who can change the levels, contrast, etc. in Photoshop.

Formatting a Book

Formatting a book for self-publishing is not as hard as it seems, especially if you gradually add to it after each case. The sections you will need to have are: main title page, table of contents, basic team information, case title page, case, and contact information.

Every book starts with a main title page. This should provide a book title, your team name, the printing term such as *2013* or *Winter 2013* or even *Summer 2013, Vol. 5*, and your city and state.

The table of contents should provide a list of investigations with their associated page numbers. This will allow people to find a particular case from a particular printing term.

It helps to include a brief 1-page team bio with a list of current team members. New readers will have a little background on the team and everyone will know who was on the team during the printing term. Team members need to disclose their names to prevent their cases becoming nullified.

For each case, provide a case title page. This should have a case name, possibly a case number, a location, and an investigation date. This should be on its own separate page. Following the case title page, you will need to have your case. Start with the summary report, followed by individual reports, gathered research, transcripts of interviews and audio, scientific analysis, maps, and media files. For each case, you will need to provide a case title page along with a case.

Definitely include your contact information since social media outlets, email addresses, team members, and the team's physical location can all change. Use this as a way to advertise for your group, include any conventions or fairs that your group will be at over the next few months, meetings that the public can attend, or any training sessions available.

Where To Publish

Scour the internet for self-publishing websites. The current popular presses are: Lulu Press, Self-Publishing, XLibris, iUniverse, Outskirts Press, and Infinity Publishing. These are usually free to sign up with and they usually offer layout or design help.

Editor's Note: Alaska Dreams Publishing (www.alaskadp.com) offers publishing consulting services or may consider publishing your books.

Chapter 8 Quiz

Define

Client Results

Public Results

Questions

1. Why are there two separate types of results?
2. What goes into the client results?
3. What goes into public results?
4. Who would want to see the client's results?
5. What do you do with your public results?
6. Why should you publish public results?

Chapter 9 - Who's Who & What's What

The following is a brief guide to some people, famous ghosts and hauntings, and other information that you should be familiar with as a ghost investigator. The listing is important for historical and cultural reasons. You will find the listings in alphabetical order. These listings are simply brief summaries. Your own research into each listing is highly encouraged.

Amityville House – The house at 112 Ocean Avenue in Amityville, New York has a well-known haunting thanks to the 1979 film *The Amityville Horror*. The book that the film was based on, *The Amityville Horror, A True Story*, was written by Jay Anson in 1977. The book and film both follow the Lutz family through their 28 day stay at their new house. 13 months prior to the Lutz' moving in, on November 13, 1974, Ronald DeFeo jr shot and killed 6 members of his family in the house. Since the release of the book and a handful of films, there has been controversy over the idea that someone would make a profit off of such a tragic and horrifying event. In 2000, DeFeo jr claimed that the murders had simply been cold-blooded murder and that claims of a haunting was false.

Dan Aykroyd – Dan Aykroyd is a well-known comedian, actor, singer, scriptwriter, and paranormal expert. Many ghost investigators claim that it was the 1984 film *Ghostbusters* that instigated their love for ghost investigation. Aykroyd has been in many films that deal with ghosts and other paranormal wonders; he has also been the host of *Psi Factor*, a television show from 1996-2000 that highlighted paranormal investigation, and *Dan Aykroyd Unplugged on UFOs*, a documentary from 2005. Dan Aykroyd also wrote the introduction for his brother's book *A History of Ghosts: The True Story of Séances, Mediums, Ghosts, and Ghostbusters*.

Art Bell – Art Bell started out as an AM political talk show host in 1978 on his own show called *West Coast AM* on KDWN in Las Vegas, Nevada. The name was changed to *Coast to Coast AM* in 1988 to encompass a larger audience. By 1995, Art Bell had migrated from the political format to being focused on issues he thought were important, conspiracies, and the paranormal. By 1997, *Coast to Coast AM* was the highest-rated late-night talk show in the United States. Art Bell retired from *Coast to Coast AM* as the main host in 2003, his replacement being George Noory. http://www.coasttocoastam.com/

Ghost of Jeremy Bentham – Jeremy Bentham lived from February 15, 1748 to June 6, 1832 in London, England. He was one of many enlightened thinkers of his time, mainly being known as the father of Utilitarianism. He believed in equal rights for men and women, the abolishment of slavery, separation of church and state, the extension of individual legal rights, and other modernist thought. Upon his death, he left in his will that his body be donated for dissection for a public anatomy class at the University College London. If this wasn't weird enough, his skeleton and head were kept, stuffed, and put on display for all to see in a box called the *Auto-Icon*. Patrons can view the sitting figure of Jeremy Bentham any day of the week. Students and professors have reported the ghost of Jeremy Bentham roaming the halls, sometimes even bowling with his head.

William Peter Blatty – Blatty is the author of the 1971 novel *The Exorcist*, which was turned into the very popular film *The Exorcist* in 1973. The novel was based on actual events and people, though the story was fictional. Father Merrin was based on British archaeologist Gerald Harding, who excavated the Dead Sea Scrolls. The exorcism itself was based on one that was performed by fr. William Bowdern. The case of possession itself was based on a young boy from Cottage City, Maryland who was subjected to an exorcism in 1949.

Madame Helena Petrovna Blavatsky – In 1875 Madame Blavatsky opened the Theosophy Society in London, England. She defined theosophy as "the archaic Wisdom-Religion, the esoteric doctrine once known in every ancient country having claims to civilization". Her major pieces of work were *The Secret Doctrine* (1888), *Isis Unveiled* (1877), and *The Key to Theosophy* (1889). She was highly influential on spiritualism and magic societies of the time.

fr. William S. Bowdern – The father's work as a Catholic exorcist, especially in the case of Roland Doe, was the basis for the exorcism in William Blatty's novel *The Exorcist*. He was also featured in the 2000 TV-film *Possessed*, in which he is played by Timothy Dalton.

Barbara Brennan – Barbara Brennan worked for NASA as an atmospheric physicist before continuing her education, obtaining Ph.D.'s in philosophy and theology. She opened up a private practice and her own school, the Barbara Brennan School of Healing, in 1982. The school focuses on the human energy field. Students can graduate with a professional studies diploma or a bachelor's of science diploma. Brennan has written two books about her healing work *Hands of Light* (1987) and *Light Emerging* (1993). http://barbarabrennan.com/

"Bloody" Mary – This is a popular children's game of calling up the spirit of Bloody Mary. Typically it's done by gazing into a mirror and repeating the name Bloody Mary three times, though the rules can change from place to place. Some believe that Bloody Mary was killed in a car accident, while others believe that she died in childbirth, was murdered, was a witch, or died in some gruesome manner.

Borley Rectory – Borley Rectory is known as the most haunted house in England after Harry Price investigated in 1937. It was built in 1863 and was destroyed by fire in 1939. The house was noted for having ghostly footsteps, the spirits of 4 people roaming the halls, a phantom carriage, strange noises and lights, and poltergeist-like activity. The investigation of Borley Rectory was the highlight of Harry Price's career as a ghost investigator.

Brown Lady of Raynham Hall – Raynham Hall lies in Norfolk, England and became famous in 1936 when the magazine *Country Life* ran a photograph of the Brown Lady, one of the most famous photographs of an apparition in the world. Investigators believe that the brown lady is the spirit of Lady Dorothy Walpole, who wore a brown dress in a painting and was the sister of Robert Walpole, the first prime minister of England. There were many reports of the brown lady, but sightings stopped after 1936.

Sylvia Browne – Sylvia Browne is a noted psychic who began her psychic career in 1974. She has authored several books and has appeared on many television shows. Controversy has graced Browne's life as many people believe her to be a fraud. Despite the fraud claims, she still remains a popular psychic. http://sylviabrowne.com/

Edgar Cayce – Edgar Cayce was known as "the sleeping prophet". He would place himself in a trance-like state in order to answer spiritual, medicinal, and historical questions. He notably remarked on natural medicine and Atlantis. He is regarded as an amazing top-notch psychic.

The Color of Ladies – Apparitions of women are sometimes noted for being a certain color, particularly: white, green, blue, and grey. Many ghost investigators believe that these colors determine the type of spirit at hand. White indicates ladies of nobility who died in a tragic way. Green ladies are often viewed as messengers of bad news or death.

Grey ladies are thought to have died for their love of someone or by the heartless actions of a family member or lover. Blue ladies were often the victims of murder and scandal.

Aleister Crowley – Crowley was a prominent occultist, author, and founder of Thelema, a spiritual philosophy based around Ancient Egyptian methodologies. He is one of the most popular members of the Hermetic Order of The Golden Dawn, even after his death in 1947. While he is not directly associated with ghosts, he is tied to psychics and rituals that could potentially unleash ghosts.

John Dee – John Dee lived from 1527-1608 and served many roles, including as a consultant to Queen Elizabeth I. He was a magician, an astrologer, an astronomer, a mathematician, navigator, and believer of Hermetic philosophy. After meeting Edward Kelley, a fellow occultist, in 1582 he became driven towards the supernatural. He produced several written pieces on occult matters.

Eastern State Penitentiary – Eastern State Penitentiary, or Cherry Hill, was built in 1829 in Philadelphia, Pennsylvania. It was in operation until 1971 and is known for having held some of the most notorious criminals in American history such as Al Capone, William Sutton, and Joe Buzzard. The penitentiary claims ghost cats, prisoners, sounds, and objects moving on their own. It is believed to be one of America's top haunted locations.

Flying Dutchman – This is the most well-known phantom ship in the world. The Flying Dutchman story was thought to originate from the 17th century when Captain Vanderdecken of the Dutch East India Company was returning home from to Holland from the East Indies. In order to accomplish this, he had to travel around the Cape of Good Hope. As legend goes, the captain swore that he would take his ship to Table Bay despite anything that God could throw at him. The ship hit an uncharted rock and sank, killing the entire crew.

In another version of this legend, the captain had gone mad and was faced with mutiny by his crew. The captain, under great stress and paranoia, saw a black figure appear on the ship and shot at him. The black figure spat a curse to the captain and crew, condemning them to eternity on the oceans, never making port, before disappearing.

The Flying Dutchman has been seen all over the world, in every ocean. It has inspired music, literature, films, and art. To superstitious sailors, the Flying Dutchman is a bad omen.

The Fox Sisters – The three Fox sisters, Leah, Margaret, and Kate, were key players in the creation of the spiritualist movement in the 19th Century. They reported ghostly rapping in their home in New York. As the sisters became more aware of the noise, they began to ask questions to the ghosts with one tap for "yes" and two for "no". The sisters began holding group sessions where they would ask the spirits questions for their neighbors to witness.

Gettysburg – The Battle of Gettysburg was a 3 day battle in Gettysburg, PA during the Civil War. It is often thought of as the turning point of the Civil War. Ghosts are seen so often in this area that it is considered to be one of the top haunted areas in America. There were around 50,000 casualties just during this battle and most ghost investigators believe that these spirits do not realize that they are dead.

The Ghost Club – The Ghost Club was formed in London in 1862 and is generally thought to be the oldest paranormal society in the world. The club began to gather in 1855 at Trinity College, Cambridge, but officially began in 1862. The Ghost Club created other venues of paranormal investigation such as the Society for Psychical Research and the American Society for Psychical Research. Members have included Charles Dickens, Sir Arthur Conan Doyle, Harry Price, Algernon Blackwood, Peter Cushing, and Peter Underwood. http://www.ghostclub.org.uk/

Holidays of Interest – There are many holidays that focus on the veil between the living and the dead being thin. The three most popular holidays are Halloween, Day of the Dead, and Walpurgis Night.

Walpurgis Night – April 30/May1. Walpurgis Night is exactly 6 months from Halloween. It is typically celebrated with a bonfire, dancing, eating, and a celebration of the supernatural. In some cultures there is a burning of a witch effigy, a parade of ghosts, and masked gatherings.

Halloween - October 31. Halloween, also known as All Hallows Eve and Samhain, is a celebration that is supposed to honor the dead. Jack O'Lanterns, carved pumpkins, are used to scare spirits from the house. Bonfires are another popular way to ward off spirits at this time. Since the dead could, on this day, mingle with the living, frightening costumes were worn to avert the spirits from attaching themselves to the living. Seances, ghost stories, and food banquets featuring apple and pumpkin are other popular occurrences on this day.

Day of The Dead – November 1. This Mexican holiday is in connection with All Souls Day and All Saints Day. The Day of The Dead is a holiday where the dead are honored. It is celebrated with song and dance, but also by creating an alter for the dead where food, flowers, and objects are left. Sugar skulls are a popular sweet item created and eaten during this time. Often times there are trips to family grave sites where items may be left for the dead.

Hans Holzer – A well-known paranormal researcher from Austria. Holzer wrote his famous book *Ghosts* in 1997, but also authored over 100 books, plays, and film scripts. He was a key investigator on the Amityville house in New York. He also taught parapsychology at the New York Institute of Technology.

Harry Houdini – Harry Houdini was an illusionist, escape artist, magician, and stunt man. He was also a strong believer in afterlife communication. Houdini was known for going to mediums and clairvoyants debunking the frauds, making him appear highly skeptical. His wife, Bess, held a séance in an attempt to contact Harry from the afterlife. It is said that she lit a candle that night that burned for ten years in Harry's memory.

Peter James – Peter James was a well-known and respected psychic from the Phoenix, Arizona area. He was known, not only for his psychic ability, but also for his great compassion with those he helped. Peter James wrote many books and appeared on many television shows.

William Mumler – (b. 1832 – d. 1884) William Mumler is the grandfather of spirit photography. He was an amateur photographer. After developing a photograph of himself, he found that there was a second image of a person in the photograph with him; it was his cousin, dead for 12 years. Mumler soon became a full time spirit photographer capturing photographs of the ghost of Abraham Lincoln, among others.

Ludwig Lavater – (b. March 4, 1527 – d. July 5, 1586) Ludwig Lavater was a prolific Swiss author of religious and demonological works. His most popular piece was *De Spectris, Lemuribus Et Magnis Atque Insolitis Fragoribus (The Ghost, The Great Unknown)*, written in 1569. It was translated into many languages and widely distributed.

Harry Price – (b. January 17, 1881 – d. March 29, 1948) Harry Price was a British author and paranormal investigator. Price was predominately interested in magic, psychic phenomena, and spiritual activity. Price investigated Helen Duncan's claims of producing ectoplasm. Price wrote 12 books on his research.

RMS Queen Mary – The Queen Mary began its life in 1936 as an ocean liner on the Cunard-White Star line. During WWII the ship was used as a transport for troops. It was painted grey and became known as "The Grey Ghost". After WWII she was reinstated as a passenger liner once more. The ship was retired in 1967 and docked at Long Beach, California. Today she is a museum, hotel, and tourist attraction. Many ghosts are said to haunt the ship, including a little girl, military men, and past passengers.

The Spiritualist Movement – In the 1840s, there was growing interest in the supernatural, especially with spiritual communication. The spiritualism movement exploded with interest when the Fox sisters from Rochester, NY began to hold public sittings as they asked questions to a spirit in their house. Leaders in the spiritualist movement were predominately women. The main movement died out around the 1920s, though there are still spiritualist groups active today.

Star Gate Program (CIA) – The Star Gate program went on from 1970 to 1995 and revolved around psychics. The psychics were "remote viewers", essentially psychics so in-tune that they could spy on other countries with their mind. It has been suggested that the Russians, Chinese, and a few other countries had similar psychic warfare programs set up. The Star Gate program inspired the book and 2009 film *Men Who Stare At Goats*.

Rev. Montague Summers – (b. April 10, 1880 – d. August 10, 1948) The Reverend was an expert on demonology, witchcraft, vampires, and werewolves. He provided the first translation of the *Malleus Maleficarum* in 1928. While he was a member of the Catholic clergy, he was severely interested in the occult and was friends with Aleister Crowley. The Reverend wrote 8 books on the occult, was the author on many other books, and was the editor or translator for at least 17 books.

TAPS – The Atlantic Paranormal Society (TAPS) was founded by Jason Hawes and Grant Wilson as a way of networking with other paranormal investigators. In October 2004, TAPS was given its own television show on the Sci-Fi channel called *Ghosthunters*. The television show led to public awareness, many similar paranormal-reality shows, and an increase of amateur ghost investigators. http://the-atlantic-paranormal-society.com/

Troy Taylor – Troy Taylor is a supernatural historian, an occultist, and author of more than 96 books. He founded the American Ghost Society in 1996 and is based out of Illinois. He is a noted public speaker and has also been featured on many radio and television shows. http://prairieghosts.com/

Ed & Lorraine Warren – The Warrens have been working as demonologists for more than fifty years. They have even been called in to deal with some of the worst outbreaks in recent times. They founded the New England Society for Psychic Research (NESPR) in 1952 with the main goal to investigate hauntings. They have appeared on many television shows. http://www.warrens.net

Waverly Hills Sanitarium – Located in Louisville, Kentucky, Waverly Hills was a very large tuberculosis hospital that opened in 1910. In the 1960s it switched names to WoodHaven Medical Services and also switched practice from tuberculosis to geriatrics, since a cure for tuberculosis had been discovered. The hospital was closed in 1980. The hospital currently is considered one of the top haunted places in America. http://www.therealwaverlyhills.com/

John Zaffis – Zaffis has been a paranormal investigator for over 37 years and currently has his own museum of haunted objects. Based in Connecticut, Zaffis runs the Paranormal and Demonology Research Society of New England, founded in 1998. He has been featured on many television and radio shows, including his own television show *The Haunted Collector*. http://www.johnzaffis.com/

Bibliography

If you are looking to create a library of books for your ghost investigations, I recommend the following. This is a list of all the books listed in the chapters, plus the books that you should own that are not listed. Books are listed alphabetically by author name.

Bayless, Raymond. *Apparitions and Survival of Death.* University Books: New York, 1973.

Brennan, Barbara. *Hands of Light: A Guide to Healing Through the Human Energy Field.* Bantam Books: New York, 1988.

Brennan, Barbara. *Light Emerging: The Journey of Personal Healing.* Bantam Books: New York, December 1993.

Buckland, Raymond. *Buckland's Book of Spirit Communications.* Llewellyn Publications: St.Paul, 2004. Third edition.

Calmet, Rev. Fr. Dom Augustin. *Dissertations Upon The Apparitions of Angels, Daemons, and Ghosts, and Concerning the Vampires of Hungary, Bohemia, Moravia, and Silesia.* ECCO Printing: London, 2010. Reprint of M. Cooper, 1759 edition. Reproduced from the British Library. Translated from French.

Gaukroger, Stephen. *Objectivity: A Very Short Introduction.* Oxford University Press: Oxford, 2012.

Giraldo, Mathias de. *Histoire Curieuse Et Pittoresque Des Sorciers.* B. Renault: Paris, 1846. Reprint. French.

King James I. *Demonology.* Filiquarian Publishing: United States, 2006. Reprint.

Konstam, Angus. *Ghost Ships.* The Lyons Press: Connecticut, 2005.

Ledwith, Miceal and Klaus Heinemann. *The Orb Project.* Atria Books: New York, 2007.

Liddell, Samuel and MacGregor Mathers, translators. *The Goetia. The Lesser Key of Solomon the King.* Weiser Books: Maine, 1995.

--*The Key of Solomon the King*. Weiser Books: Maine, 2000.

Mariechild, Diane. *Mother Wit*. The Crossing Press: California, 1987.

Markowitz, Mike. *EVP: Electronic Voice Phenomenon*. Schiffer Publishing: 2009.

Offutt, Jason. *Darkness Walks: The Shadow People Among Us*. Anomalist Books: San Antonio, 2009.

Rose, Carol. *Giants, Monsters, & Dragons. An Encyclopedia of Folklore, Legend, and Myth*. W. W. Norton & Company: New York, 2000.

--*Spirits, Fairies, Leprechauns, and Goblins. An Encyclopedia*. W. W. Norton & Company: New York, 1996.

Summers, Montague. *The History of Witchcraft & Demonology*. Alfred A. Knopf: London, 1926.

Webster's New World Dictionary and Thesaurus. Michael Agnes, Editor in Chief. Hungry Minds, inc: New York, 2002. 2nd edition.

Wilson, Colin. *Poltergeist! A Study in Destructive Haunting*. G.P. Putnam's Sons: New York, 1982.

Index

Appendix I

Objectivity Exercises

Please use the following exercises in a group setting. Have an open group discussion. There is no right or wrong answers. Be sure to have a copy of the question available for the whole group to see. Keep in mind the following question: How would you stay objective with an approach or a case like the following?

1. A 35-year old woman approaches your team at a San Francisco paranormal convention where you have a booth set up. She tells you that she had a dream where she was terrorized by a black demon with glowing yellow eyes. The woman discloses that she recently had a close relative die and that she is not very religious, but her parents were both Baptist. When this woman woke from her dream she had found a bunch of standing pictures, a vase, a few light-weight lamps, a handful of trinkets, and few pieces of china fallen over. How do you approach this case? Is there anything special you might want to do?

2. Your team is approached by a sobbing older couple who claim that they have a possessed grandson. They provide you with pictures of the boy (a school picture and two pictures of his suspected possession) and they show you a short video on their cell phone of him in his suspected "possessed" state. They tell you that they are Jewish and that they believe that this all started with an old mirror that they received as a gift. How do you approach a case like this? Is there anything special you might want to do?

3. A small-town medium claims that she can communicate with the dead and has even had ectoplasm appear during some séances, though she doesn't have any samples with her. How do you approach a case like this? Is there anything special you might want to do?

4. A dead-looking tree in the woods has been called "The Wolf Tree" due to an old native legend that a great wolf spirit died under the tree. As the legend goes, the great wolf spirit was so angry with the one who killed him that a curse was placed on the land surrounding the tree so nothing would grow and nothing would survive in that area. A conscientious business man wants to purchase the land that the tree is on to build some homes. How do you approach a case like this? Is there anything special you might want to do?

5. A new, overly excited team member brings in their first case: a young military guy who claims that a demon is physically abusing him. Your new team member shows the team pictures taken of a few scratches on the man's chest and neck, as well as a "mystery" bruise on his ribs. The new member is absolutely sure that this soldier is being tormented. How do you approach a case like this? Is there anything special you might want to do?

Appendix II

Investigation Forms

The following forms are easy to use and will be needed for every investigation. Please copy them from your copy of this book or visit http://alaskadp.com for online files.

Privacy Form – This form will protect you and your client from each other. It's very general, but it clearly establishes the level of privacy you need to keep with your client. Any client and witness you have for a case will need to sign this form.

Client Statement Form – This form is a basic statement form, but you will need to have paper ready for your clients who have a lot of information to share.

Interview Questionnaire – This 3-page form is for the investigator doing the interview only. It is designed to help collect information. Questions are provided with space for long answers.

Editor's Note: The above forms can be downloaded for free at the author's page on the ADP website: http://www.alaskadp.com.

Privacy Form

Date_____

Case #_____

I, _____(print name), request
to keep the following information private from future forms
of information sharing in the following manner:

Mark all that apply.

☐ You can reveal all details about my case.

☐ You can reveal information about the case, but do not
use information in which could result in strangers
contacting me (street address, phone number, email,
etc).

☐ Please refrain from using my real name. Please use the
following pseudonym: _____
(print false name)

☐ Please cover my face, unless absolutely necessary, in
any printed visual material.

☐ You can use my name and my personal information,
but leave out the personal information for the
following person(s).

**Client
Signature**_____

I understand that anyone under the age of 18 will only be
named by a first name, unless otherwise noted above, and
their personal information will be extremely limited to only
necessary information for the case in an effort to protect their
individual rights and privacy.

Initial_____

If you wish to give permission for information to be shared
about a child under the age of 18 for the purpose of public

sharing, where the case will be presented in a printed journal format for the purpose of tracking case similarity and sharing incidents, please note the child's name and age, your signature, and the child's signature.

Child's Name (print)_____ **Age**_____

Child Signature_____

Parent/Guardian Signature_____

I serve as witness to the signing of this privacy form. **Date**_____

Investigator's Signature_____

Client Statement Form	**Date**_____
	Case #_____
Sighting Location_____ _____	**Sighting Date**_____
Time of Sighting ____:____AM/PM	**# of Witnesses** _____

I verify that the information here is true.

Client
Signature_____

Clearly write about your encounter. Use as many pieces of paper you need for your statement. Please include full names and contact information of other witnesses, if possible.

Interview Questionnaire (For Investigators Only) Investigator Name_____ Client Name_____	Date_____ Case #_____
Location of **Sighting/Address**	**Contact Information for Client**
Time(s) of Sighting	☐ Reoccurring or ☐ Isolated Sighting?
Smells Were any smells present during the sighting? More than one smell? Was there anything strange about the smells? More Information:	**Sounds** Were any sounds present during the sighting? Were the sounds responsive to client's actions? If voices are reported, are they male or female? More information:

Case #	
Visuals	**Actions**
Was anything seen with the naked eye? Refer to Chapter 3 for terminology.	Did objects move around?
	Was anyone injured in any way?
	Were there drastic changes in temperature?
Was anything seen through media like photos or video? (Obtain a copy.)	Was there any sudden movement to the air?
	Are the actions of the ghost directed at one particular person?
Did any foreign objects randomly appear?	
Animals	**Children**
Were any animals affected?	Were any children directly affected?
Were any animals injured? Are there any animals currently in harm's way?	Were there behavioral changes to any children?
Were there behavioral changes to any animals?	

Case # _____	
Location History	**Client History**
When was the location established?	Was your client(s) using any occult items like a ouija board or spells?
Who last owned it? (If a house was built by your client, ask about the land.)	What is the background of your client?
	Profession:
	Age:
Is there a violent history of the location?	Moved Recently?
	Relationship status:
Anything strange about the surrounding area like an old family burial plot, a spot where nothing will grow, etc?	Family status, if any:
	Client's Religion:
	Client's Place of Worship:
	Stress in life outside of sighting?
	Other information:
What was the weather like during the sighting?	
Any prior sightings by other people at location?	

About the Author

Jessie Desmond was born in Fairbanks, Alaska in 1982. Growing up, regular family activities included cooking, hiking, fishing, camping, and playing scrabble with the family at dinner. Her interest in the paranormal and occult started as early as she can remember, starting with ancient Egypt, ghost stories, and vampires. She has been investigating the paranormal and the occult since 1999. She has two university degrees, one in 2D Animation from the Joe Kubert School in New Jersey and the other in History from the University of Alaska.

Other titles by Alaska Dreams Publishing
www.alaskadp.com

Currently available:
Inside the Circle
Ghost Cave Mountain
The Silver Horn of Robin Hood

Upcoming Titles from Alaska Dreams Publishing:
A Coming Storm
Through My Eyes
The Adventures of Jason and Bo
From Ranch to Rails

Personal Notes Section

The following blank pages can be used to take notes.

www.ingramcontent.com/pod-product-compliance
Lightning Source LLC
Chambersburg PA
CBHW070959040426
42443CB00007B/575